SHINING STAR QUILTS

LONE STAR VARIATIONS

with Sunbursts, Broken Stars, Blazing Stars, and more

JUDY MARTIN

 **M.Q.M.**

Moon Over the Mountain Publishing Company
6700 West 44th Avenue, Wheatridge, Colorado 80034-0394

ACKNOWLEDGMENTS

Special thanks to Pat Martin and Steve Bennett for all the jobs, large and small, they took on to help me complete this book. Thanks also to Bonnie Leman and Louise O. Townsend for letting me bounce my ideas off them. Thanks to all the people at my local quilt shops, who knew just what I wanted when I described fabric over the phone, who mailed it to me or took it home for me to pick up after hours, and who knew when to leave me alone and when to offer suggestions. A big thank-you goes to the dedicated staff of quiltmakers who turned my ideas into the wonderful quilts you see in this book: Brenda Bain, Roberta Brown, Irene Couchon, Reni Dieball, Wendy Dodge, Jeanette Goodrich, Shirley Ann Holbrook, Pat Magaret, Marilyn Michael, Louise Morrison, Linda Nolan, Carol Sears, Geri Waechter, Maryneil Walker, Daphne Wells, Janet Yates, and Marty Youngblood. Finally, thanks to the generous people who cooperated in lending photographs for inclusion in the book: Marie Anderson, Robert Bishop, Mary Dillon, Sandi Fox, Dr. and Mrs. Donald Herr, Glendora Hutson, Barbara Janos and Barbara Ross, Michael Kile, Emiko Toda Loeb, Mrs. John Loeb, Cyril Nelson, Bets Ramsey, Lelah Sewell, Merry Silber, and Shelly Zegart.

Photographs by Jerry DeFelice
Production Assistance by Andrew H. Leman and Mary Ellen Schwenk

©Copyright 1987 Judy Martin
Published by Moon Over the Mountain Publishing Company
6700 West 44th Avenue, Wheatridge, Colorado 80034-0394
Library of Congress Card Catalog Number 87-91259
ISBN 0-943721-00-8
First Printing 1987

CONTENTS

INTRODUCTION

The Lone Star quilt has been a favorite for over two hundred years. The graphic impact of one grand star is certainly part of the appeal. The design is bolder and less repetitious than most quilt patterns, and the possibilities for subtle color effects are especially attractive. In studying old Lone Star quilts, I became enchanted by the great variety of effects achieved by quilters who worked with the Lone Star pattern in the past. In fact, the Lone Star is not just a pattern, it is a whole family of patterns. Unfortunately, modern-day quiltmakers haven't been tuned in to the creative possibilities of the Lone Star. I think they're missing out on a lot of fun, so I decided to write this book in order to share some of the inspirations and techniques that will allow quilters today to enjoy the Lone Star as much as our foremothers did.

Over the years, Lone Stars have remained a popular, recognizable pattern group while they have encouraged creative variations. Perhaps superstition accounts for some of the urge to embellish the pattern. In some parts of the country, a Lone Star was considered an unlucky gift, as the solitary star was seen to symbolize a solitary future. However, a Lone Star *variation* – with additional stars pieced into the background for example – would be received with pleasure. Superstition aside, there are plenty of other arguments for varying the basic star. It's always satisfying to add your personal touch to a quilt. Moreover, Lone Stars invite innovation. The star begs for unique color treatments. The large background patches call out for embellishment. The legacy of Lone Star quilts made in the past provides a precedent and plenty of inspiration. Once you've seen a few of the possibilities for variation shown in this book, you'll be anxious to try your hand at rearranging the parts or adding pieced borders to personalize your Lone Star quilt. You'll soon realize that the Lone Star has as much potential for design variation as the ubiquitous Log Cabin.

Some quilt historians seem to think that Lone Stars were reserved for "best quilts" because they were so difficult. I have another theory. In the first place, as a quiltmaker myself I can testify that Lone Stars are not so difficult to sew. I think that beauty was more a factor than difficulty in determining which quilts were to be best quilts. It seems likely to me that Lone Star quilts became best quilts because they were so impressive. Their grand proportions provided graphic strength and a perfect space for extravagant quilting. Furthermore, when fine quilting was lavished upon them, they looked worthy of it. They commanded the respect of recipients, who may have had no idea about what constituted a difficult pattern.

While the Lone Star isn't the easiest quilt to make, it shouldn't intimidate any quilter. Even a beginning quiltmaker can handle it with a little guidance. And you'll find all the technical help you desire in this book. If you are interested in designing your own Lone Star, you'll find inspiration plus design suggestions, yardage charts, diamond templates, and more. If you prefer to make the patterns as shown, you can skip over the design material and charts and be satisfied with the complete pattern instructions and basic quiltmaking information. You'll find that the patterns are full size with seam allowances, grain lines, and specially designed quilting motifs. You'll be interested in the helpful hints provided with each pattern, and you'll want to look over the Quick Piecing Methods chapter and the Special Piecing Tips, which are full of practical information about making Lone Stars. Step-by-step photos will guide you in the most efficient methods for making Lone Stars.

With the new shortcuts, helpful tools, and quick techniques described in this book, it is possible to make a basic Lone Star quilt top in a day and an elaborate, full-size quilt top in just about a week's time. What I find puzzling is why any quiltmaker would spend her time making anything less impressive than a Lone Star.

HISTORY

NAMES

Lone Star quilts have been known by many different names over the years. The earliest examples were most often called Star of Bethlehem, although Rising Sun was another name often connected with the pattern. The name Lone Star probably didn't surface until the mid-1800s, when the annexation of Texas was a political issue. Texas Star, Lone Star of Texas, and Star of Texas are other variants of this name. Blazing Star and Bursting Star are occasionally seen to name the pattern, and some regional names, such as Amherst Star in Ontario, Canada, persist. Among contemporary quiltmakers, "Lone Star" is by far the most widely used name for the pattern today. For this reason, I have chosen to use "Lone Star" in this book for describing a basic star quilt made up of many diamonds.

Related patterns may have several names, as well. Sunburst is also known as Diamond Star and Eternal Star; Broken Star is sometimes called Bursting Star; and quilts of many small Lone Stars are called by a number of names. Some of these names are: Harvest Sun, Star of the Bluegrass, Prairie Star, Ship's Wheel, Blazing Star, Star of the East, Star of David, and Touching Stars. Some of these names identify specific variations; others are used more generally.

I am including Sunbursts, Broken Stars, Harvest Suns, and other related patterns in this book of Lone Star patterns because, like Lone Stars, these patterns are made from units formed of many diamonds. Historically, Lone Stars have been treated to many unique variations; I believe the Sunbursts, Broken Stars, and Harvest Suns to be just variations on the arrangement of Lone Star parts. These are simply side trips in the exploration of Lone Star possibilities.

ORIGINS

The Lone Star pattern appears to have originated after 1776. Lone Star quilts dating from the fourth quarter of the 18th century are among the earliest remaining examples of quilts as we know them. Because these early quilts were heavily embellished with applique and embroidery, each example was highly individualized. The possibilities for variation in Lone Stars were well explored by early quiltmakers. However, these early examples share certain characteristics with each other and with other quilts of that period. These oldest quilts are consistently large, often exceeding 120 inches square. They are styled after the popular Indian textiles of their period, with a central medallion framed by one or more distinctive borders. The quilts are elegant, decorated with *broderie perse* (finely appliqued print cutouts) or sometimes embellished with elaborately pieced motifs in the background squares and triangles. Typically, fanciful chintz borders or elegant pieced or appliqued borders were used to surround the large central star.

A GRAND TRADITION

It is not surprising that the earliest remaining quilts should be so grand. For them to have survived so long, they must have been treasured, indeed. A significant number of Lone Star quilts dating from the end of the 18th century remain intact. Perhaps this was considered the pattern of choice for someone wishing to make an heirloom quilt. Or perhaps this quilt, once made, was so impressive as to command the kind of respect bestowed upon an heirloom. Conceivably, the Lone Star may have enjoyed such great popularity at the end of the 18th century that it was a statistical inevitability that this pattern should be among the few patterns represented in quilts still remaining from that period. In any case, the Lone Star must have been a highly regarded pattern then, and it remains so to this day.

Lone Star quilts have changed somewhat over the years, reflecting the prevailing styles. Nowadays, quilters seldom embellish their stars with *broderie perse,* for example. Very little has been written specifically about Lone Star quilts and the way they have evolved. In order to have some understanding of these quilts, I undertook to catalogue the 191 different, dated examples I found in 53 books and museum or exhibition catalogues (listed in the bibliography on pages 142-144). I recorded dates, sizes, numbers of diamonds, the kind of material from which the diamonds were cut, the backgrounds, borders, and arrangements. While I realize that my secondhand information and the relatively small size of my sample body do not make for the most accurate and complete findings, I feel that my survey results bring up some interesting possibilities. In fact, they suggest some trends that are consistent with more scholarly studies on the subject of quilts in general. Keeping in mind the casual nature of my survey, let's look at some of the results in the context of quilt history.

Arrangements. The current thinking about early quilts is that central medallions styled after Indian palampores predate block-style quilts. In my survey, of the ten examples made before 1825, eight were Lone Stars and two were Sunbursts, both medallion styles. It was not until the second quarter of the 19th century that quilts of many small, block-size stars first appeared. From 1825 to 1875, surveyed Lone Stars outnumbered quilts of many stars by a factor of almost three to one. Between 1875 and 1900, the two arrangements enjoyed equal popularity. In later years, the many-starred quilts again declined in numbers. The peak of popularity for the many-starred (block) arrangement occurred just when sewing machines were becoming widely available. This supports the view of scholars who suggest that the sewing machine made the block style a viable and attractive alternative to the old central medallion style.

The first Broken Star in my survey appeared around 1900. Perhaps it was the sewing machine and the spirit of experimentation spawned by it that led a quiltmaker somewhere to develop this long-lived variation. The Broken Star could easily have evolved out of the Dutch Rose block. Once blocks and block variations were commonplace, a quiltmaker might have seen the Lone Star as simply a big LeMoyne Star with many little diamonds. It is a small jump from there to the idea of making a Broken Star, which is just a single, quilt-size Dutch Rose block of many little diamonds. (See the illustration on page 13.)

Fabrics. What other trends are suggested by my survey? It seems that the early examples used printed fabrics exclusively for the diamonds. The first examples in my survey to use solids for the diamonds were dated after 1825. Gradually, the use of solids gained popularity. By the third quarter of the 19th century, solid diamonds had a slight edge over print ones. From 1900 to 1950, solid diamonds were favored almost three to one over print diamonds. The use of print diamonds has enjoyed a renewed popularity since 1950, though, being used about twice as often as solids since that time.

Fillers. Background squares and triangles were anything but plain in early Lone Star quilts. It was in the background areas that quilters most often expressed their individuality by inventing pieced or appliqued embellishments for the basic star. Of the ten surveyed quilts made before 1825, only one had a plain background. Six had squares and triangles embel-

SURVEY OF CHANGES

CHRONOLOGY AND TRENDS

lished with *broderie perse.* One had an elegant chintz background, one was done in applique, and one was pieced. After 1825, backgrounds were less often done in *broderie perse.* Plain backgrounds grew steadily in popularity. Fully one-third of the examples from 1825 to 1875 had plain backgrounds. This style peaked between 1925 and 1950, when 19 out of 20 Lone Stars in the survey were made with plain, solid-colored backgrounds. Even now, solid fabrics remain the most popular choice for background squares and triangles.

Borders. Lone Stars dated before 1825 were consistently trimmed with borders. Borders were pieced, appliqued, or cut from elaborate chintz. Often, several different borders graced a quilt. From 1825 to 1850, half of the examples had no borders at all or had plain strips of fabric for borders. Most of the remaining examples had pieced borders or elaborate chintz borders. Few were appliqued at this time. By 1900, even more of the quilts— three-fourths of them—had plain borders or none at all. The plain or unbordered style peaked between 1900 and 1925, when only one quilt out of the 17 surveyed had pieced borders. None had appliqued borders. Since then, pieced borders have made a bit of a comeback, although plain borders remain the most common today.

Summary. Early makers of Lone Star quilts seemed to revel in adding personal touches to the basic star design. At first, they concentrated on borders and background fillers. By the early 19th century, they were experimenting with arrangements, as well, adding the Sunburst and the many-starred arrangements to their repertoire. In recent decades, quiltmakers seem to have forgotten the exciting potential for variation in the Lone Star pattern. The quilts made in the first three quarters of the 20th century display a disappointing uniformity. However, a few contemporary quiltmakers are now beginning to explore the Lone Star pattern once again, treating it with imagination.

Possibilities. With this book, I hope to open quilters' eyes to the wonderful possibilities for personalizing Lone Star quilts. Perhaps I can in this way contribute to a revival of the spirit that inspired our foremothers to make the delightful, innovative Lone Stars we see in books and museums. By looking backward, perhaps we can gain insights for taking strides ahead.

PLANNING

JUST ENOUGH PLANNING TO ADD A PERSONAL TOUCH

You may not consider yourself a designer, preferring to make your Lone Star from one of the patterns in this book. Still, it is very likely that you will be adding some personal touches to your quilt. Perhaps you'll decide to change the colors somewhat. Before you start your quilt, give this chapter a glance. You'll see just how easy it is to be creative with your Lone Star. You'll get ideas for different color schemes as well as ideas for borders, background quilting, and more.

GETTING REALLY CREATIVE

The graphic impact of a Lone Star is always impressive, and the fabric selection and color choices let you exercise your own creativity. But this can be just the beginning of the fun in store for you. If the idea of designing your own quilt appeals to you, you will want to read this chapter carefully. It is full of ideas for being creative with Lone Stars. You may not have realized the versatility of the Lone Star—its great potential for design variation. The possibilities for different arrangements, background motifs, borders, and diamond substitutes are truly exciting. Even if you have never designed a quilt before, you should be able to parlay one or more of these simple ideas into a beautiful and distinctive Lone Star that will make you feel like an accomplished quilt designer. Let's look at these design elements one at a time to help you see the possibilities for your own Lone Star.

ARRANGEMENTS

Arrangements from the Past. Long ago, quiltmakers discovered the versatility of the Lone Star and reveled in rearranging its parts. Some variations have been around for a hundred years or more. Sunbursts and quilts of many small Lone Stars have been made since at least the second quarter of the 19th century. Many of these quilts look surprisingly different from their Lone Star cousins. All have been made using diamond-shaped blocks made up of many smaller diamond patches. Here are a few arrangements gleaned from antique quilts.

Lone Star

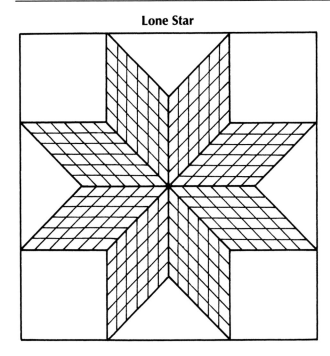

Touching Stars

Expanded Star

Garfield-Arthur Quilt

Blazing Star

Sunburst

Arrangements Inspired by Traditional Blocks. Think of the Lone Star as a great big LeMoyne Star block. The two designs are shown side by side below for comparison. The Lone Star, as you can see, is just a bed-size star made up of eight diamond-shaped star points. Each of the star points, in turn, is made up of many smaller diamonds.

Similarly, a Broken Star quilt may be thought of as a great big Dutch Rose block, with its diamond-shaped star points made up of many smaller diamonds. These two designs are also shown below.

This thinking can be carried further to suggest dozens of new arrangements for star points made up of many smaller diamonds. All sorts of traditional blocks suggest themselves as possible arrangements. In fact, any block with diamond patches becomes a candidate. A few possibilities are: Stars and Cubes, Love in a Mist, Poinsettia, Mother's Choice, and Farmer's Daughter. Three of the quilts in this book were designed from blocks such as these. See the quilts on pages 46 and 55.

Study the illustrations below and on page 14 to see more examples of the lovely quilts that can result from adapting traditional blocks into arrangements for Lone Star units.

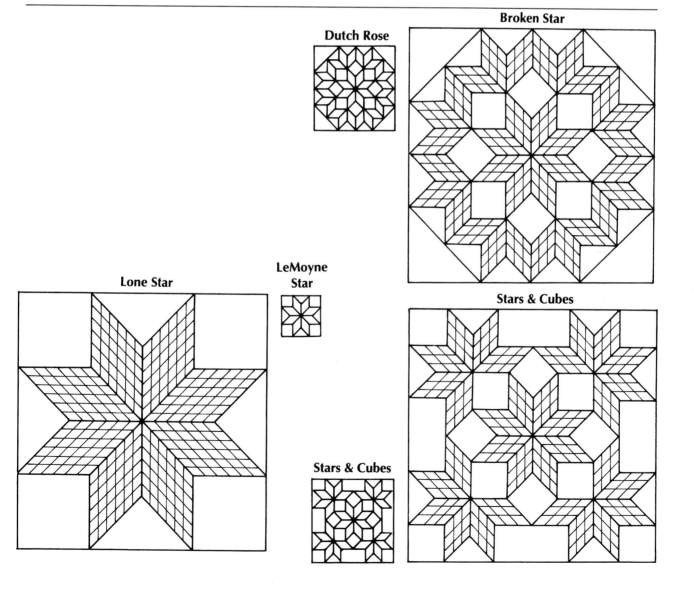

Dutch Rose

Broken Star

Lone Star

LeMoyne Star

Stars & Cubes

Stars & Cubes

Love in a Mist

Poinsettia

Mother's Choice

Farmer's Daughter

Flying Swallows

Rolling Star

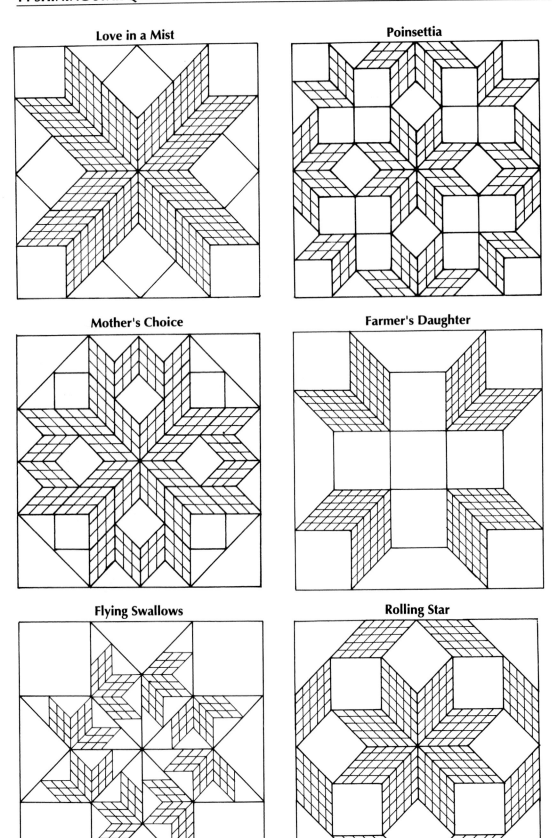

Original Arrangements. With all of these possibilities for Lone Star arrangements to inspire me, I couldn't resist trying my hand at designing some arrangements of my own. A few of these are shown below. Feel free to play with Lone Star arrangements to suit yourself, as well.

Radiant Star

Grand Star

Spring Star

Lancaster Rose Star

Rectangular Arrangements. Most of the Lone Star arrangements form square quilts. While these make lovely wall quilts or king-size quilts, depending on the size and number of diamonds, what do you do for a twin or double bed?

I put my mind to adapting arrangements into rectangular shapes, and I came up with a number of interesting solutions. The Sunrise Star and Twinkle, Twinkle, Little Stars quilts shown on pages 49 and 56 are just two examples. I am sure that you, too, can design a pleasing arrangement for a twin or double bed. Start by studying the examples below and on page 17.

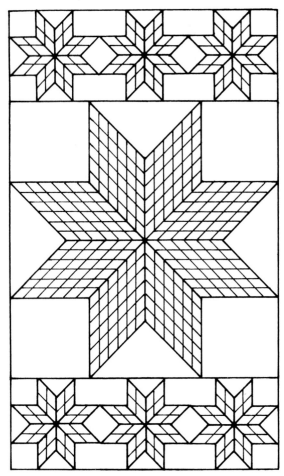

Lone Star bed quilts are often made with one large star extending from edge to edge of the quilt. However, I feel that a Lone Star quilt looks better and creates more of a focal point if the star lies almost entirely on the top surface of the bed. When the points drop very far over the sides of the bed, the star cannot be seen whole from any point of view. A star of about 39" for a twin bed, 54" for a double bed, 60" for a queen bed, and 72" or 78" for a king bed would fit the top surface perfectly. However, quilts in these sizes would look small and silly on the appropriate-sized beds. You'll need an additional ten or twenty inches beyond the star to cover the pillow area and to form a drop at the sides and bottom of the bed. A twin-size quilt might range from about 60" x 85" to about 80" x 95". A double quilt might be somewhere between 72" x 84" and 96" square. A queen-size quilt should be about 80" x 90" to 100" square. And a king-size quilt should be about 94" square to about 118" x 100", depending on the bed and the desired drop. The diagrams below show some workable formats for Lone Star quilts to fit specific bed sizes.

QUILT SIZES AND FORMATS

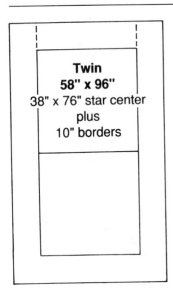

Twin
58" x 96"
38" x 76" star center
plus
10" borders

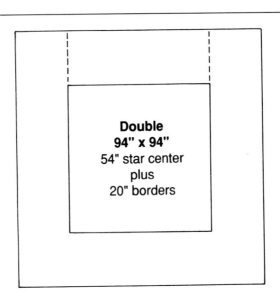

Double
94" x 94"
54" star center
plus
20" borders

Queen
100" x 100"
60" star center
plus
20" borders

King
96" x 96"
72" star center
plus
12" borders

Expanded Lone Star designs such as the Broken Star (page 43) offer a natural way of completing a bed-size quilt with a central star that is no larger than the top of the bed. Broken Star quilts have one star on the top surface of the bed and another ring of star points that drape over the sides to form a self-border. Other examples of self-bordering arrangements are on pages 47 and 55.

BORDERS

The Broken Star idea suggests a solution for other arrangements, as well: Simply add borders to complete the quilt. A wide, extravagantly quilted border would be one way of finishing a Lone Star to look good on a bed. A beautiful appliqued vine or swag might be another attractive way of finishing a small Lone Star for use on a bed. Perhaps the most natural way of finishing a Lone Star quilt is to add a pieced border incorporating the same diamond patches that are in the central star.

Lone Stars were first made as medallion-style quilts surrounded by one or more elaborate borders. See examples of these early, medallion-style Lone Stars on pages 35 and 36. Because Lone Stars have long been considered "best quilts," it is not uncommon to find lovely pieced or appliqued borders adorning even recently made quilts. The quilts on pages 41, 42, and 45 are good examples of old and new quilts with pieced borders.

Pieced Borders. Among the favorites are borders pieced of diamonds. These take many forms, some of the prettiest of which are shown below. Each is shown with single diamonds, although these may be made up of four or nine diamonds (or more) if desired. The diamonds can be the same size as those in the central star, and the borders often require no additional pattern templates.

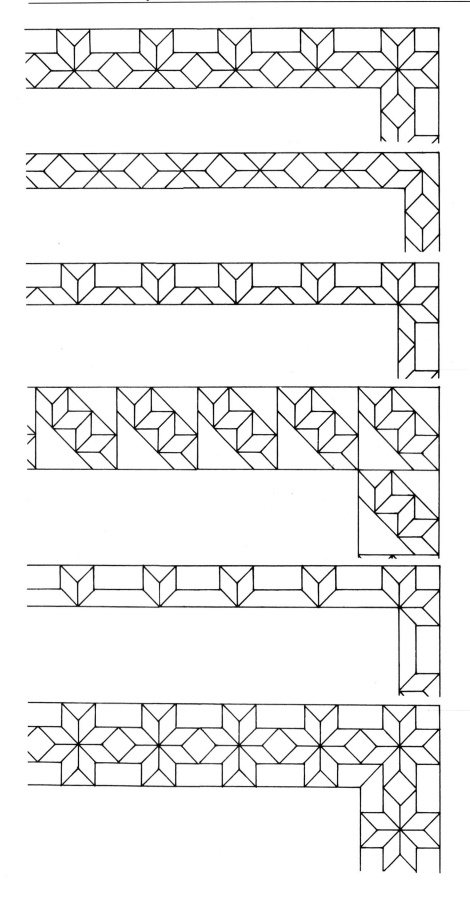

Borders for Square Quilts. Most Lone Star quilts are square in shape with equal borders surrounding the square center. This makes border planning especially easy. Any border can look attractive and well thought out if you are careful to do two things: First, you must center the border motifs the same way on all four sides of the quilt. And secondly, you must miter the corners. Below you can see how much better the same border looks with mitered corners rather than butted corners.

Pieced Border, Butted Corners: Poor

Pieced Border, Mitered Corners: Good

Pieced Borders Related to Stars. Some borders made from the same diamond patch that is used for the Lone Star will naturally fit a true Lone Star, even without plain strips. These are pieced designs that share the unique spatial properties of Lone Stars. Whole stars and half stars are the most obvious examples, although many other arrangements of diamonds plus squares, rectangles, and triangles also qualify. Several of these special motifs are on page 20. In each case, the number of border units that will fit along each side of the star will exactly match the number of diamonds per row in the Lone Star point. You will need something extra for the border corners, often another whole motif or half motif for each corner. In some cases, you may want to slide the motifs over by a half unit for a better corner treatment. Study the example at the top left on page 22. The Lone Star has six diamonds per row in each star point. Six border units fit the Lone Star exactly. These could be arranged with six half stars on each side and quarter-stars in the corners. However, I preferred to slide the motifs over by a half unit to make more attractive corners.

Pieced Border Related to Stars

Wider Pieced Border Related to Stars

Wider Versions of the Related Borders. Here is an attractive border alternative for those of you who are comfortable dealing with a little computation. If you would like to use one of the borders from page 20 but you have in mind something wider, you can make any of these borders with four, nine, or more diamonds in place of each one in the motif. This will make the background squares, triangles, and rectangles larger, as well. If you use four diamonds for each one shown (two rows of two diamonds), the border will be twice as wide. If you use nine diamonds (three rows of three diamonds) for each one, the border will be three times as wide as the single-diamond version. The larger border will fit the Lone Star perfectly if you keep in mind one rule: The number of diamonds per row in the Lone Star points must be divisible by the number of diamonds per row you are using to replace each diamond in the border. See the example above right. The half-star border here has four diamonds per star point rather than just one. There are six diamonds per row in the Lone Star and two diamonds per row in the border units. Six divided by two equals three, the number of border units that fit along one side of the Lone Star.

Pieced Borders Plus Plain Strips. Sometimes, borders such as those on page 19 look best with whole motifs and a little flourish at the corners. In most cases, you will have to add a plain border strip between the quilt center and the pieced border for a good fit. If you like math, you can work this out at the planning stage. If you prefer a more direct approach, you'll still have to do a little arithmetic and some measuring, but the idea is pretty straightforward: Simply make the border a little longer than the quilt center, measure both parts, and divide the difference between the measurements by two. The result is the width of plain border strip needed, not including seam allowances. Examples of this idea can be found on pages 35, 36, 51, and 53 as well in the first figure on page 23.

Pieced Border Plus Plain Strips

Borders for Rectangular Quilts. Some borders will not look very good on rectangular quilts. Even with a plain strip inserted between the star and the pieced border, it may be impossible to achieve matched corners when the sides of the quilt are longer than the top and bottom edges. See the rectangular quilt below left. However, if you select one of the special borders on page 20, it is possible to achieve a very handsome border for a quilt center that is the width of a Lone Star and twice as long. This is a good proportion for a twin bed, and the border units relate to the length of the quilt as well as the width for a perfect fit on each side of the quilt.

Pieced Border for Rectangular Quilt: Poor Corners

Pieced Border for Rectangular Quilt: Good Corners

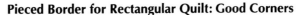

The basic Lone Star has a background of four large corner squares and four edge triangles. In other arrangements the sizes, shapes, and quantities of background patches may vary. Still, in all except the Sunburst arrangement there will be large patches of background material. Nowadays, these patches are usually showplaces for fancy quilting. However, in antique Lone Stars, piecing or applique frequently embellished these background patches. See the antique quilts on pages 33, 35, 36, and 38-42.

Most of the contemporary quilts in this book have quilted background patches. Echoing Star, page 50, and Flying Star, page 48, are good examples. A few of the contemporary quilts have pieced backgrounds. Mariner's Star, page 47, is one such quilt. Spring Star, page 52, with its pieced flower blocks, is another example. A couple of the contemporary quilts have appliqued fillers. Country Rose Star, page 54, has appliqued flowers in the background, as does Star of Love, page 46. A variety of ideas for filling in background patches follows. Some of the motifs are original and others are from antique Lone Star quilts.

BACKGROUND MOTIFS

Quilted Background Motifs

Pieced Background Motifs

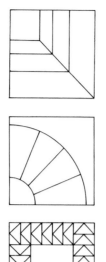 

Appliqued Background Patches

The patches making up each Lone Star point need not be just uniform diamonds. For interest, it is fun to combine small and large diamonds, diamonds and parallelograms, or diamonds and half-diamond triangles, among other shapes. Many of the Lone Star quilts in this book are made from diamonds in combination with other shapes. Flying Star, page 48, has parallelograms, as does Starburst, page 50. Gem Star, page 52, has small and large diamonds, as does Fanciful Star, page 48. The combinations and recombinations add delightful variety to the possibilities for Lone Star quilts. Following are just a few of the many possible combinations of diamonds with other patch shapes. Use your imagination to come up with other combinations as well.

**DIAMONDS
AND VARIANTS**

Rings. Most Lone Star quilts are made with concentric rings of color radiating from the center. The eight center diamonds form the first ring. A second fabric is used for the sixteen diamonds forming the next ring. A third fabric is used for the twenty-four diamonds in the following ring, and so on. Notice the concentric rings of color in the Lancaster Rose Star quilt on page 54.

Repeats. Frequently, after the widest ring the fabrics repeat. The repeat might be 1-2-3-4-3-2-1 or it might be 1-2-3-4-1-2-3, or even 1-2-3-1-2-3-1. In the outer star points of the Mariner's Star quilt on page 47, the repeat is 1-2-3-4-5-1-2-3-4-5-1.

COLORING AND FABRIC SELECTION

Rings	Repeats
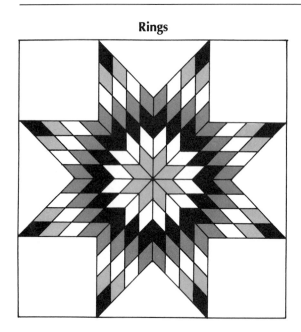	

Checkerboards. Sometimes, a checkerboard effect is desired, and every second ring is made of white diamonds to match the background. This gives a strongly graphic effect if the colors have good contrast. The sequence here might be 1-2-3-2-4-2-5 or 1-2-3-2-3-2-1 (where 2 is white). The Prairie Star quilt on page 34 and the Star quilt on page 40 are good examples of checkerboard effects.

Concentric Stars. For an interesting effect of stars within stars, the Lone Star can be colored not in rings but in concentric stars, as shown at the top of page 29. Since several touching diamonds will be the same color, it helps to have a variety of prints and fabrics in each color family. For this reason, the concentric-stars color idea is best executed in scrap fabrics. The block on the right of the second row of the Twinkle, Twinkle, Little Stars quilt on page 56 is an example of this type of coloring. Another variation of this idea can be seen in the Radiant Star quilt on page 53. Here, there are just two concentric stars, each made of many diamonds. The diamonds are colored in the typical rings up to the line dividing the inner and outer stars.

Checkerboards

Concentric Stars

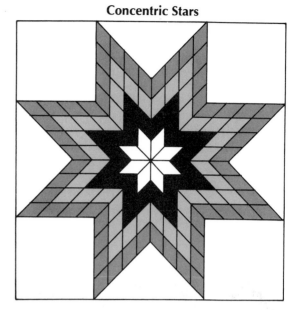

Alternating Star Points. Star points can be colored two different ways, with the two types of points alternated. This idea would be attractive with various shades of red in one point and various shades of blue in the next, for example. The two kinds of points could have the same light/dark sequence for continuity. Another way of using alternating star points is illustrated in the Wreathed Star quilt on page 46. Four of the center star points are darker colors than the other four. Each uses the same sequence of colors, but with different shades of these colors in the two types of star points.

Color Chains. The colors can even be organized in lengthwise chains similar to an Irish Chain idea. This is illustrated below and in the outer edge blocks of the Wreathed Star quilt on page 46.

Alternating Star Points

Color Chains

Color Bands. Here, star points are colored in rings, but the colors repeat rhythmically with one color flanked on both sides by the same color. The sequence might be 1-2-3-1-3-2-3. This creates a wider band of color. The Rising Star quilt on page 35 and Star of Bethlehem on page 39 are examples of this color variation.

Accents. The Lone Star can be made with the center diamond of each ring of a star point colored in a strong, contrasting accent color. This theme can be used in conjunction with almost any of the other color effects. Two examples of this idea are the Echoing Star on page 50 and the Unfolding Star on page 55. The accent color might be placed in a variety of other positions in the star point. It could be only in the inner rings or in all rings except one, for example.

Color Bands	**Accents**

Other Effects. These are just a few ideas for organizing the color in your Lone Star quilt. I am sure that you will think of many other creative solutions. The Twinkle, Twinkle, Little Stars quilt on page 56 illustrates a number of interesting color arrangement ideas in its various blocks.

Blending and Contrast. Colors can be chosen to blend into one another gradually, or they can be selected for contrast. I prefer color sequences that use both blending and contrast to form wide and narrow bands of color, blending together in some places and defining distinct areas elsewhere. In the Sunrise Star quilt on page 49, various shades of a color blend, but where green touches blue or pink touches green, for example, the contrast is strong.

Spaces. The visual effect of "spaces" in the star can be created by coloring a ring of diamonds to match the background. By coloring the widest ring in this way (see the Radiant Star quilt on page 53), the star points seem to be detached from the center, so that they appear to float in space.

For another effect, match the innermost diamonds to the background to make a star-shaped space.

Match the next-to-the-last ring to the background for another interesting effect, where the star tips seem to twinkle, appearing connected and detached at alternate moments. (See the Earth & Stars quilt, page 51.)

Match just a few diamonds to the background for a notched effect. Two of the blocks in the Twinkle, Twinkle, Little Stars quilt on page 56 are notched like this.

For just a suggestion of a space, cut some diamonds in fabric similar in color to, but not exactly the same as, the background fabric. These diamonds will appear as spaces one moment and as bona fide rings of color the next moment. This effect can be seen in the light print triangles of the Gem Star quilt on page 52.

Scraps. Scrap fabrics can be used instead of carefully matched yardage. A couple of examples are the Bursting Star and Log Cabin Star quilts on page 38. With scraps, you'll want a color scheme that includes at least two, and perhaps several, colors. That way, you can use a variety of red prints to form one ring and brown prints to form the next, for example. The color contrast will be sufficient for the rings to show up, yet you can use a variety of shades for the scraps within a ring. A monochromatic color scheme would be more difficult to handle successfully with scraps.

Color Sequence. The particular sequence of colors and prints in a Lone Star is largely a matter of personal taste. You can color a drawing with felt pens or colored pencils to preview your plan, but it is a good idea to remain flexible about the exact sequence until you have actually selected fabrics for it. Sometimes the fabric will suggest a different arrangement. Perhaps two fabrics will look so pretty side by side that you'll decide to change the sequence.

Work from your own fabric stash or augment your fabrics with yardage bought especially for the quilt. If you are working with small pieces of fabric, you'll want to keep in mind that the smallest pieces will have to be used for the innermost or outermost rings (the ones with the fewest diamonds).

I don't like to lock into a particular fabric sequence at the quilt shop, so I buy ³/₄ yard of anything that I think I'll use and take it home to decide on the exact position. Three-quarters of a yard is enough for most rings and is not so much that I can't afford the leftovers for future projects. I try to make my decisions about sequence soon after I get home from the store so that I can buy additional yardage as needed before the store runs out of it.

Judging the Effect. It is helpful to prewash and dry the pieces of fabric you are considering and fold them into uniform-sized pieces. Stack and stagger the fabrics in any order you desire, with the folded edge of the bottom piece extending an inch or two beyond the next piece, and so on. When you have the right number of fabrics neatly spread out this way, stand back and judge the effect. Make any adjustments. Consider both the overall effect and the individual interactions of neighboring fabrics. Try to have a variety of types and scales of prints, especially from one patch to its neighboring patch. Do you have some areas of strong contrast and other areas of blending?

Preferences. I have found some patterns of contrast and blending to be more pleasing to me than others. For example, I often make the eight center diamonds contrast sharply with the next ring of sixteen diamonds. This is a matter of personal taste, and you are sure to have preferences of your own, once you think about color placement in Lone Stars. Study the photos in the book. Do you like a strong, well-defined star in the center, as in the Spring Star on page 52, or do you prefer an ever-expanding, blended

Sunburst in the center? Do you like repetition as in the Mariner's Star, page 47, or do you prefer unrepeated rings of color as in the Lancaster Rose Star, page 54? Do you like blended star points as in the Country Rose Star, page 54? Strong color at the widest ring as in Unfolding Star, page 55? A checkerboard effect as in the Prairie Star quilt, page 34? Do you want to use "spaces" as a visual effect as in the Earth & Stars quilt on page 51?

Once you have settled on a fabric sequence, you may want to cut out some diamonds (enough for about three star points) and arrange them to see how you like the developing pattern. Don't be afraid to try a few adjustments. Sometimes you need to see the diamonds together to know for sure what looks best. If you will be strip piecing your Lone Star, you can cut out a few diamonds if you have fabric to spare, or you can skip this step, relying on the stacking and staggering of folded fabrics described earlier. When you have worked out an arrangement that you like, record the sequence of fabrics on a sheet of paper. Number the fabrics and cut a swatch of each. Use the yardage figures listed for your pattern, or look up the necessary yardage in the appropriate chart. Make sure you have enough of each fabric before you proceed with the quilt.

PLATE I. Star of Bethlehem, 93" x 94½", circa 1850, New England. Photo courtesy of E. P. Dutton, Inc. This stunning quilt has wonderfully elaborate pieced background squares and triangles. Tiny Lone Stars and LeMoyne Stars sparkle in an impeccably planned arrangement. The intricacy and grandeur of this quilt as well as the colors recall the impressive Lone Stars of the late 1700s.

PLATE II. Prairie Star, 72" x 83", circa 1880, Kentucky. Made by Judy Ann Scott. Photo courtesy of Kentucky Quilts. Every third ring of diamonds matches the background, creating a checkered effect. Note how some diamonds extend through the corner squares.

PLATE III. Star Variation, 68" x 75½", circa 1865-1870, Kentucky. Made by Virginia Bland Smith. Photo courtesy of Kentucky Quilts. This quilt is a Sunburst, an early favorite. The diamonds expand in ever-widening rings rather than tapering to points.

PLATE IV. Star of Bethlehem, 82¼" x 84¼", circa 1885, Pennsylvania. From the collection of Pilgrim-Roy. Photo courtesy of Sandi Fox. A typical Lone Star is raised out of the ordinary by the simple addition of an unusual green frame to vibrate against the red.

PLATE V. Star of Bethlehem, 80¾" x 81¼", circa 1890, Pennsylvania. From the collection of Pilgrim-Roy. Photo courtesy of Sandi Fox. Quilts of many Lone Star blocks were especially popular around the time this quilt was made. Note the use of scraps.

PLATE VI. Rising Star, 104" x 104", circa 1820. Photo courtesy of Dr. Robert Bishop and E. P. Dutton, Inc. This quilt is typical of the style of Lone Stars from the last quarter of the 18th century through the first quarter of the 19th century. The applique cutouts in the *broderie perse* style, the elaborate print and pieced borders, the central medallion styling, and the use of chintz for the diamonds are seen in many examples from this period. The arrangement of the diamonds into this crisscrossed pattern is unique, however. The pieced border in this example is especially handsome, with thoughtfully planned corners.

PLATE VII. Star of France, 78" x 79", circa 1930, a Home Arts Studio pattern. Photo courtesy of E. P. Dutton, Inc. This design has its diamond patches arranged uniquely to form a handsome four-pointed star. The use of solid-color fabrics was typical of Lone Star quilts of the period. Fan-like pieced motifs embellish the areas between the star points.

PLATE VIII. Star of Bethlehem, 114" x 117", circa 1840, Kentucky. Photo courtesy of Kentucky Quilts. This quilt of chintz and fine cotton has the large size, embellished background, and multiple pieced borders typical of earlier Lone Stars. Note the interesting corner treatment in the outer pieced border.

PLATE IX. Sunburst, 69$^{1}/_{2}$" x 78$^{1}/_{4}$", circa 1840, Photo courtesy of E. P. Dutton, Inc. This arrangement of diamonds is nearly as old as the Lone Star pattern. In this notable example, rather than continuing the diamond pattern into the corners, the quiltmaker chose to complete her quilt with pieced-and-appliqued corner triangles. A simple strip of pieced diamonds finishes the top and bottom edges of the quilt.

PLATE X. Bursting Star, 82½" x 84", 1861-1865, Stewart County, Tennessee. Made by Timexenia M. Morris Roper. Photo courtesy of The Quilts of Tennessee. A stunning Lone Star in carefully sorted scraps is made unforgettable by the addition of over 200 tiny stars pieced together to form the background squares and triangles.

PLATE XI. Garfield-Arthur Quilt, 85" x 85", circa 1880, Pennsylvania. Photo courtesy of Shelly Zegart's Quilts, Louisville, Kentucky. A printed bandana from the presidential campaign of 1880 forms the centerpiece of this unusual quilt. While the quilt contains no diamond patches, it provides a unique example for arranging Lone Star units (see page 12).

PLATE XII. Log Cabin Star, 76" x 80", circa 1890-1900, Kentucky. Made by Ellen Smith Tooke Vanzant. Photo courtesy of Kentucky Quilts. Large diamonds are string pieced of small, irregular-shaped scraps, providing a refreshing randomness.

PLATE XIII. Star of Bethlehem, 72" x 72", circa 1920, from the Ohio Amish. Photo courtesy of Barbara Janos and Barbara Ross. This striking Lone Star features an unusual pieced-and-appliqued background of stars in circles.

PLATE XIV. Star of Bethlehem, 90³/₄" x 92", circa 1849, New York. Made by Elizabeth E. Moseman. Photo courtesy of E. P. Dutton, Inc. Over 4,000 tiny diamonds make up this winning design. Note the interesting sequence of colors, with light and dark in alternating rings and many of the dark rings flanked on both sides with the same fabric. This makes pleasing bands of color. The filler squares and triangles are embellished with pieced Sunburst sections. An elaborate print border adds the finishing touch.

PLATE XV. Star, 79" x 79", circa 1876, Kentucky. Made by Robert Toupe. Photo courtesy of Kentucky Quilts. This quilt is an excellent example of a Lone Star in a checkered coloring. Every second ring is white to match the background. Red diamonds radiate from the center to the Star tips, and blue diamonds fill out the rings. A single red LeMoyne Star is appliqued in the center of each background square or triangle. The overall effect is most energetic.

PLATE XVI. Rising Star, 82" x 82", circa 1850-1860, New England. Photo courtesy of Merry Silber. The Lone Star with smaller stars in the background squares and triangles is a popular New England variation. In many examples, the color rings repeat as they do here. An inner sawtooth pieced border and a pretty floral stripe give this quilt its distinctive look.

PLATE XVII. Star of Bethlehem, 91" x 93", circa 1840. First published in *The Quilt Digest 1.* From the collection of Dr. and Mrs. Donald M. Herr. Photo by Sharon Risedorph. Courtesy of The Quilt Digest Press, San Francisco. This elegant Lone Star is embellished with applique wreaths and floral corners as well as sawtooth edging and handsome diamond borders. Geometric and natural forms pair beautifully here. The sequence of diamonds in the star forms triple bands of green-yellow-green and red-white-red for an interesting, formalized effect. This quilt was planned with the utmost care to achieve a perfect fit between the feather-edged blocks and the star as well as between the quilt's center and its pieced borders. Notice how applique is used in the border corners to echo the applique in the background squares and triangles.

PLATE XVIII. Star, 70" x 70", circa 1860, Kentucky. Made by Fannie Sales Trabue. Photo courtesy of Kentucky Quilts. This silk-and-velvet Lone Star borrows style elements from its 18th-century predecessors. The pieced border and appliqued background squares and triangles recall the chintz quilts of the 1790s. However, the choice of colors and materials gives this quilt a very different look. The elegant fabrics and dark colors anticipate the Victorian crazy quilts so popular twenty years after this quilt was made.

PLATES XIX-XXII. Four Broken Star quilts, each 108" x 108", 1985-1986. Designed and made by Lelah Sewell; quilted by the Amish. These are just a few of the many Broken Star quilts made by Lelah, who enjoys working with fabric and often takes her color cues from nature. It is apparent that Lelah enjoys using color to achieve different effects from the same pattern.

She uses a variety of background colors, from very light to strong and bright. The rings of diamonds blend in carefully gradated shades. She varies the placement of the lightest and darkest rings for somewhat different looks. Some of the diamonds match the background fabrics to create the illusion of spaces in the design, adding sparkle to the quilt.

PLATE XXIII. Star of Bethlehem, 53" x 53", 1980, designed, pieced and appliqued by Glendora Hutson; quilted by Gayle Larson. Graded colors in cool and warm hues blend and contrast in this contemporary example. The quilt pays homage to the traditional form, yet the jaunty colors and the clean-lined simplicity of the appliques reflect current tastes.

PLATE XXIV. Misei, 85" x 61", © 1986, by Emiko Toda Loeb. This sophisticated contemporary quilt incorporates three-plus stars in an unusual asymmetrical arrangement. The background, pieced of low-contrast purple diamonds, is reminiscent of a Sunburst, but with a very different effect. Strip piecing embellishes the star points. An elegant reinterpretation of a classic form, this quilt with its moody darks and electric accents is a perfect example of a Lone Star variation reflecting contemporary sensibilities.

PLATE XXV. Summer Mountain Morning, 116" x 116", © 1985, designed and made by Mary Evangeline Dillon. The main design of this quilt is simply a Lone Star pieced of eight star points, each made from 19 rows of 19 diamonds. The effect of a central lake surrounded by eight pine trees, in turn surrounded by eight mountain peaks, is strictly a matter of color placement. Fine quilting and a handsome border of pieced pine trees and stars complete this contemporary masterpiece.

PLATE XXVI. Wreathed Star, 58" x 58", 1987. Patchwork and quilting designed and fabric selected by the author. Pieced by Wendy Dodge. Quilted by Daphne Wells. The arrangement is based on a Rolling Star block. The small half-star blocks in the corners add an interesting finishing touch. The main star is colored with four light and four dark star points, creating a shaded, practically three-dimensional effect. At the same time, the star appears to have the traditional rings of color. In order to achieve both the ringed effect and the light/dark effect, fabrics for each ring have been chosen carefully in two shades just a step apart. The outer eight diamond-shaped units are colored in lengthwise chains rather than rings. This pattern begins on page 89.

PLATE XXVII. Star of Love, 58" x 58", 1987. Design and fabric selection by Judy Martin. Made by Louise Morrison. In this quilt, the eight star points are separated by appliqued blocks. What a pretty way to avoid having eight points come together! The lightest peach print in the widest ring of the star points nearly matches the background. This serves to detach the inner half of each star point from the outer half. The background spaces are filled with quilting in a heart motif to echo the appliques. You will find the pattern for this quilt on page 129.

PLATE XXVIII. Mariner's Star, 102³/₈" x 102³/₈", 1987. Piecing and quilting designs plus fabric selection by Judy Martin. Pieced by Brenda Bain; quilted by Shirley Ann Holbrook. A cross between a Broken Star and a Mariner's Compass, this quilt is a real attention-getter. A medley of nautical quilting motifs embellishes the large background areas. A simple palette of six fabrics was used to keep the quilt from looking overly complicated. One-quarter compass blocks fill the squares between the star points, and they add a pleasing scalloped effect to the central star. The Mariner's Star pattern starts on page 118.

PLATE XXIX. Fanciful Star, 55½" x 55½", 1987. Patchwork and quilting design and fabric selection by the author. Stitched by Maryneil Walker. Softly graded colors in rainbow sequence, interrupted occasionally by a darker accent, make a particularly radiant Lone Star. Large diamonds, small diamonds framed on two sides with narrow strips, and half-diamond triangles are combined to form a bordered star. Fan blocks fill the background squares, repeating the rainbow colors with a graceful, fluid touch. The pattern starts on page 96.

PLATE XXX. Flying Star, 52⅛" x 52⅛", 1987. Design for piecing, quilting, and fabric sequence by Judy Martin. Sewn by Marty Youngblood. The most basic of Lone Stars is made even simpler here by substituting parallelograms for groups of diamond patches. The idea was inspired by the Liberty Star quilt block. A woven effect is created in the center of the star. At the tips, the pattern slips back into the more usual diamonds. Fabrics from a pastel rainbow imbue the pattern with a gentle, yet colorful, spirit. The pattern is on page 100.

PLATE XXXI. Sunrise Star, 84¹/₄" x 103¹/₄", 1987. Design and fabric selection by the author. Made by Carol Sears. Here's a graceful solution to the problem of adapting a square Lone Star for a rectangular quilt. The Lone Star center is elongated with "borders" on top and bottom only. A full border completes the quilt. Background colors darken progressively from the center out. Note especially the effect achieved in the center of the star where diamonds have been cut with care from a border stripe. Pattern is on page 105.

PLATE XXXII. Echoing Star, 60³⁄₈" x 60³⁄₈", 1987. Patchwork and quilting designed and fabric selected by Judy Martin. Pieced and quilted by Pat Magaret. The arrangement is similar to a Rolling Star, but the diamonds in the bordering units are placed differently. Dark green parallelograms replace pairs of diamonds to emphasize the central star. Rust diamonds march down the center of each star point. The three-eighths stars in the outer ring have some diamonds that blend and some that contrast with the leafy print squares and triangles for an interesting effect. The eight peach background squares provide a perfect place for fine quilting. This pattern is on page 86.

PLATE XXXIII. Starburst, 68" x 68", 1987. Design and fabric sequence by the author. Sewn by Linda Nolan. This quilt has a Sunburst arrangement of ever-widening rings of diamonds. Large and small diamonds provide variety. A star in the form of black parallelograms tipped with large, black diamonds appears to be superimposed on the Sunburst. In actuality, these are pieced right along with the Sunburst diamond patches. The result is a pleasant cross between Sunburst and Lone Star designs. See the pattern for this quilt on page 116.

PLATE XXXIV. Earth & Stars, 95⅝" x 95⅝", 1987. Pattern and fabric sequence designed by the author. Pieced by Roberta Brown. Not yet quilted. This quilt is arranged in a star-within-a-star format. The inner star is made from diamonds that are about ¹/₁₆" smaller than the diamonds in the outer star. This is necessary to achieve a perfect fit. The second ring of the outer star is in a fabric to match the background. This makes the gold diamonds appear to be separated from the rest. The pattern for this quilt is on page 112.

PLATE XXXV. Spring Star, 53¹/₈" x 53¹/₈", 1987. Patchwork and quilting designs plus fabric selection by Judy Martin. Pieced by Reni Dieball. Quilted by Janet Yates. The Rolling Star arrangement of this Lone Star quilt permits the use of eight background squares rather than four squares and four triangles. This set is perfect for the use of pieced blocks as background squares. Here, the blocks are pieced flowers designed by the author for *Quilter's Newsletter Magazine.* A graceful, fluid floral quilting motif softens the angularity of the design. The pattern for Spring Star begins on page 108.

PLATE XXXVI. Gem Star, 64³/₄" x 64³/₄", 1987. Piecing and quilting patterns designed and fabric chosen by the author. Stitched by Marilyn Michael. This appealing star seems to overlap its pieced border. Large and small diamonds pair up for added interest. Two rings of large diamonds are split into contrasting triangles to echo the octagon shape of the quilt. Careful blending and crisp contrast team up for a lovely effect. The pattern is on page 126.

PLATE XXXVII. Radiant Star, 98" x 98", 1987. Patterns for piecing and quilting as well as fabric selection by Judy Martin. Pieced and quilted by Daphne Wells. The star-within-a-star look here is a simple matter of coloring. A monochromatic Lone Star in various shades of red is surrounded by blue star points in a matching size. The widest ring of the blue star points matches the white background, making the sixteen blue star tips appear to float free of the rest. The use of multicolored accents in the prints adds sparkle to a basically two-color design. A narrow plain border makes it possible for the handsome pieced border to frame the quilt gracefully. You will find this pattern on page 134.

PLATE XXXVIII. Country Rose Star, 60" x 60", 1987. Design and fabric selection by Judy Martin. Stitched by Jeanette Goodrich. This quilt is made from the same pattern as the Lancaster Rose Star quilt below. The floral motif is appliqued rather than quilted here. Colors are soft and delicate for a subdued effect. You will find this pattern on page 94.

PLATE XXXIX. Lancaster Rose Star, 60" x 60", 1987. Design and fabric selection by the author. Sewn by Geri Waechter. This stunning quilt in brilliant-colored solids is made from the same pattern as the much more subdued Country Rose Star quilt above. The gradation of colors practically glows. The small central star is framed by a ring of diamonds. The diamonds in the outer ring reverse the sequence of colors in the center star, with a change from plum to orange at the tips. A pretty floral motif is quilted in the background patches. The pattern is on page 92.

PLATE XL. Unfolding Star, 97⁷/₈" x 97⁷/₈", 1987. Designed and pieced by the author. Not yet quilted. The arrangement is similar to a Broken Star, but it is based on a Stars and Cubes block rather than a Dutch Rose. Black diamonds run down the length of each star point to accentuate the division of these units into lighter and darker halves. The color shift is subtle, with light and dark halves positioned in the quilt to suggest the effect of a light shining on a three-dimensional folded star. The pattern is on page 138.

PLATE XLI (Next Page). Twinkle, Twinkle, Little Stars, 80" x 98", 1987. Patchwork and quilting designs and fabric selection and placement by the author. Sewn by Irene Couchon. Many small stars, each framed with a dogtooth border, join together in this dazzling quilt. Each star illustrates a different color effect. Notice the use of "spaces" and striped fabrics in particular. This pattern is on page 103.

QUILTMAKING BASICS ▭

In this chapter, traditional quiltmaking methods are described. Don't feel you must read every section if you don't think you'll be using all of the methods discussed or if you are already familiar with the techniques. Beginners as well as more experienced quiltmakers may prefer the quick methods for piecing discussed in the next chapter.

HAND PIECING

Lone Star quilts have long been made by hand piecing; many quiltmakers prefer to use traditional methods to make these quilts even now. The traditional methods allow for precision at a comfortable, relaxed pace. Hand sewing makes good pick-up work, allowing the quiltmaker to make productive use of her time spent waiting for appointments, watching television, talking on the telephone, and so on. Hand sewing can be done while the quiltmaker socializes with family members. It is a slow, but enjoyable, process that makes good use of odd moments of free time.

Making Templates. Trace the patterns (without seam allowances) onto sturdy but flexible template plastic and cut them out. If you prefer, trace them onto a sheet of paper and mount the paper on something stiff like cardboard; cut out the mounted templates.

Marking and Cutting. Spread out a single layer of fabric wrong side up. Place the template face down on the fabric, and mark around it with a sharp pencil. The lines you mark will be the seam lines. Leaving enough space for $1/4$" seam allowances around each patch, mark the number of patches needed. Cut out the patches, adding seam allowances by eye.

Hand Sewing. Place two patches with right sides together and align the marked seam lines. Pin at each end. Start sewing near one end of the seam line, right on the line. Take a couple of stitches back to the end of the seam line, then proceed toward the other end with small running stitches. Turn the patches over to make sure that you are staying right on the seam lines of both patches. Backstitch to secure the thread at the far end of the seam line. Continue joining patches to make rows; then join rows. When you need to cross a seam allowance, sew right up to the stitching of the seam to be crossed, keeping the seam allowance out of the way. Then pass the needle through the seam right at the stitching line, flip the seam allowance out of the way, and continue stitching on the other side of the allowance. This way, seam allowances remain free to fold to either side.

HAND APPLIQUE

Making Templates. Templates for hand applique do not include turn-under allowances, nor do the applique patterns in this book. Trace the solid outline of the patch onto template plastic or mount a paper tracing onto cardboard to make a template for hand applique.

Marking and Cutting. To mark patches for hand applique, place the template face up on the right side of the fabric. Draw around it lightly with a pencil. This marked line will be the turn-under line. Leave room for adding $3/16$" turn-under allowances by eye when you cut each patch.

Hand Sewing the Appliques. Turn under the $3/16$" allowances on each patch and baste in place. It is not necessary to turn under edges that will be tucked under other appliques. Clip into the turn-under allowance as needed for smooth curves.

Position the background block over the pattern in the book to see placement for the appliques. Pin the appliques in position.

Applique with a blind stitch in a thread color that matches each patch, not the background color. Trim away the background fabric from behind appliques after stitching each patch, if desired.

ADDING MITERED BORDER STRIPS

Measure the completed quilt top from seam line to seam line across the middle of the quilt. Measure and mark a border strip to match; there should be some extra length if everything has gone as planned. Center the border strip on one side of the quilt top, with the extra extending equally on both sides. Pin at the center and at the end marks, then pin at 3" to 4" intervals. Sew in a 1/4" seam, beginning and ending at the seam line, not at the outer edge of the fabric. Repeat for each side of the quilt.

With the quilt face down on a flat surface, smooth one border over the adjacent one and draw a diagonal line from the end of the stitching on the inner seam line to the point where the two borders cross. Switch the two borders so that the other one is now on top. Repeat, drawing a diagonal line. Match the two pencil lines with fabrics right sides together, and sew through them. Cut away the excess, leaving just 1/4" seam allowances. Press seam allowances to one side. Repeat at the other three corners of the quilt.

MARKING FOR QUILTING

Place the quilting pattern under the quilt top, aligning the motif in the appropriate space. Trace the design onto the quilt top, marking with a chalk pencil or water-soluble quilt marking pen.

Outline quilting (1/4" from the seam lines around each patch) or quilting "in the ditch" (right next to the seam on the side without the seam allowance) can be done by eye. Other straight lines can be marked with masking tape as you quilt. Simply stitch along the edge of the tape. After stitching, pull up the tape to reuse it.

LINING THE QUILT

Make a quilt lining about 4" larger than the quilt top. You may have to seam together several pieces of fabric to achieve the necessary size. Be sure to trim off selvedges before stitching. Press the seams to one side. Spread the lining face down on a flat surface. Smooth the quilt batt over the lining, being careful not to stretch it. Center the quilt top, right side up, over the batting. Pin the three layers as needed to hold them together while you baste. Baste in rows four to six inches apart; also baste around the edges.

HAND QUILTING

You can mount the quilt in a large frame or simply use a quilting hoop to keep the quilt taut as you stitch. Quilting is done in a short running stitch with a single strand of quilting thread. The stitch goes through all three layers. Use a short needle, such as an 8 or 9 betweens, with about 18" of thread. Make a small knot in the thread, and take a first, long stitch through top and batting only. Tug on the thread to pull the knotted end between the layers. No knots should show on the front or back of the quilt.

Take straight, even stitches that are the same size on the top and bottom of the quilt. For tiny stitches, push the needle with a thimble on your middle finger, and guide the fabric in front of the needle with the thumb and index finger of your hand below the quilt. To end a line of quilting, take a tiny backstitch, and then make another inch-long stitch through the top and batting only. The thread end will stay embedded in the batting better if you run the needle right between two close lines of quilting for the inch-long stitch. Clip the thread at the surface of the quilt.

BINDING AND FINISHING

Trim the quilt batt and lining even with the quilt top. Leaving about 2" extra binding at each end, place a 1 1/2" binding strip on one edge of the quilt top, right sides together. Sew through all layers (binding, quilt top, batting, and lining) with a 1/4" seam allowance, beginning and ending at the seam line. Repeat for the other three sides of the quilt. Fold the binding to the back of the quilt, tucking under 1/4", and blindstitch it down along the seam line. At the corners, trim, tuck in the ends, and stitch in a miter.

QUICK PIECING METHODS □

Even if you have your own favorite methods, you will want to look over this chapter to see if you'd like to incorporate any of these ideas into your own approach to quiltmaking. If you want just a summary of the methods, look at the step-by-step photos at the end of each section and read the brief captions. Then, if you are interested in more details on either or both of the quick methods, go back and read the appropriate sections.

Some quilters avoid the machine piecing and strip piecing techniques because they fear that their piecing will be imprecise. While it is true that some fairly sloppy quilts have been made using these techniques, sloppy quilts have also been made entirely by hand. I think that attitude, not method, is the principal factor in determining how neat and precise a quilt will be. Machine sewing can be every bit as accurate as hand sewing. And the cutting can be as perfectly aligned with the grain and print as you desire. For the greatest speed, you can cut through as many as eight layers of fabric at once. If you want individually centered printed motifs, you can cut just one layer and still save time by not having to mark. Practice is another factor in determining how well your quilt turns out. If you have done machine sewing for years, you may find that your machine work is more precise than your hand work. Conversely, if you are unfamiliar with the sewing machine, you may find it difficult to achieve an acceptable level of accuracy when you attempt machine piecing. Of course, you can always keep at it, and with time you will achieve proficiency in whatever method you prefer.

QUICK SCISSOR CUTTING AND MACHINE PIECING

If you would just as soon dispense with the marking and get on with the cutting and sewing, you'll love this method. It can be as accurate as hand piecing. And it's fast—maybe just as fast as strip piecing, once you get the hang of it. The most involved pattern in this book, the Mariner's Star on page 47, was made using the quick scissor cutting and machine piecing methods described here. It took just 42 hours to cut and piece, including prewashing and ironing the fabrics and pressing the completed quilt top. A smaller project can be made in a day or two. The Flying Star quilt top on page 48 took just 11 hours to make.

With this method you can make all sorts of Lone Star projects that can't be done by strip piecing alone: scrap quilts such as the Bursting Star or the Log Cabin Star on page 38; quilts with curved seams such as the Mariner's Star on page 47 or the Fanciful Star on page 48; quilts made with patches other than uniform diamonds such as the Echoing Star or the Starburst on page 50; quilts with non-row piecing such as the Spring Star quilt on page 52, with its unique flower blocks; and quilts made with patches cut carefully centered over a special part of the print such as the Sunrise Star quilt on page 49.

You won't need to learn a whole new way of thinking in order to piece with this method. You'll still be assembling individual patches in basically the same fashion you would use for hand piecing. And you won't need any tools you don't already have. Just a sharp pair of scissors, pins, and a sewing machine will do fine.

Making Templates. Start with a paper pattern piece. This should include ¼" seam allowances, and the points should be trimmed. A properly trimmed point will be even with the edge of the neighboring patch when the seam lines are positioned for stitching. This provides valuable clues for positioning patches that have no seam-line markings. The patterns in this book have been drafted with the points already trimmed. If you are drafting a pattern of your own design, align the tip of your pattern over a diamond from the book to trace the lines for trimming the point. Repeat at the other point. Trim the points of the background triangles as follows: Lay the diamond template (already trimmed) over the point of the triangle. Align two sides of the diamond with two sides of the triangle. Trim the triangle to match the diamond. Repeat for the other point of the triangle. Trace or draft several copies of the pattern so that you can discard them as they get ragged from use.

Planning Grain Lines. Most often, diamond patches are cut with two sides on the straight grain and the other two sides on the bias. Occasionally, grain line is ignored altogether to achieve a special effect from a printed motif. Sometimes, diamonds are cut with all four sides on the bias and the straight grain extending between the tips, although this is tricky to sew.

In order to keep your piecing smooth and unruffled, it helps to plan your grain lines so you are always sewing the straight grain of one diamond to the bias edge of the neighboring diamond. By matching the bias edge to the straight, you'll avoid stretching the bias edge of the patch as you stitch.

It is really very easy to plan for these straight-to-bias grain lines. Start by labeling one face of your diamond template "A" and the opposite face "B." Mark a grain arrow along one edge of your diamond template on the "A" face. Next, label the rings of diamonds in your Lone Star, with the first ring of eight diamonds being labeled "A." The second ring of sixteen diamonds is marked "B." The third ring of 24 diamonds is marked "A." And so on, as shown in the diagram. All of the diamonds in the odd-numbered rings are "A" diamonds; all of the diamonds in even-numbered rings are "B" diamonds. This will guarantee that every bias edge will be stabilized by an adjacent straight-grain edge of a diamond.

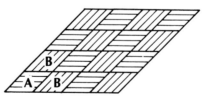

**Grain Line Planning
for Diamonds**

Observe the grain line (given on each pattern piece in the book) when cutting other patches, as well. Background squares should be straight with the grain. Cut the background triangles so that the edge of the unit, block, or quilt is on the straight grain. (Usually, the long edge of the triangle will be the straight-grain edge.) Don't cut the diamonds from folded fabric or you will get two different grain lines for patches of the same fabric.

Lengthwise grain (parallel to the selvedge) is firmer and more stable than the crosswise grain. Furthermore, printed fabrics are much more likely to be printed even with the lengthwise grain, whereas they may be printed badly off-grain in the crosswise direction. Therefore, you should plan to cut borders, strips for strip piecing, and other long patches along the lengthwise grain.

Cutting Multiple Patches Without Marking. It is possible to cut up to eight layers of fabric at one time with good accuracy. I prefer cutting four to six layers for the best combination of speed and accuracy. If you are making a quilt from just a few coordinated fabrics, you can layer different fabrics that need the same kinds of patches. Be sure to keep the grain lines even. Put the smallest piece of fabric on top to avoid cutting beyond the edge of any fabric.

For the diamonds, unfold the fabric and press it smooth. For speed, you can layer four to six different fabrics that require diamonds, pressing each layer. If you do this, put the fabrics requiring the fewest diamonds on top so that you can remove them when you have cut the number of diamonds you need. Refer to your grain line plan. Lay fabrics face up for "A" grain diamonds and face down for "B" grain diamonds. You will be cutting all of the diamonds, "A" and "B," with the "A" side up and the grain arrow aligned with the lengthwise grain of the fabric.

For background squares and triangles, fold a single fabric to make several layers for cutting. Start by folding lengthwise, the way fabric comes off the bolt, matching selvedge to selvedge. For four layers, also fold crosswise so that selvedges of all four layers are aligned. Press the fabric as you layer it. Plan to cut patches along the selvedges and raw edges first, keeping well clear of the folds of layered fabric.

It is not necessary to trim off the selvedges, but position the patches a half inch or so from the selvedge at the closest point. Position the paper pattern on the layered fabric, aligning the grain arrow of the pattern with the straight grain of the fabric. Hold the pattern in place with your fingers. Cut, moving your fingers as needed to keep the pattern in place as you cut. Use short strokes in the middle of the blades. (The tips of the scissors don't always cut smoothly, and in order to use the back of the blade you need to elevate the fabric too much, which can shift the layers.) Cut the largest pieces first. Smaller pieces can be cut from the leftovers.

Planning the Piecing Order. This book uses "exploded" block diagrams to indicate which pieces are joined first. If you are designing your own Lone Star, you will want to plan your piecing order. Often, patches are sewn into units: units are joined into rows, and finally rows are joined to make a block. Usually the last seams sewn are those that extend from edge to edge of the block. When one large patch touches several smaller ones, the small patches are almost always joined before the large patch is added. Try working backwards from the longest seams to the shortest ones to plan your best piecing order. If you have trouble planning this on paper, make a sample block and take note of how you pieced it.

Making Star Points Assembly-Line Style. Basically, assembly-line piecing involves repeating one small step over and over until that step is completed for the whole quilt. Then you go on to the next small step, repeating it for each block or star point. With this method, it takes awhile to complete one star point, but the second, third, and all the succeeding star points fall together very quickly. In fact, you can finish all of them practically at once! Because assembly-line piecing is so fast, you can repeat a mistake countless times before you know it. Therefore, it is important that you plan ahead carefully. It is helpful to lay out a complete star point, then spread it into rows. You can stack eight patches deep to lay out all eight star points in one place.

For designs with diamond variants such as triangles, parallelograms, or small and large diamonds, join all of the patches to form diamonds of a uniform size first. Then join all of these diamonds in the same manner as you would a standard Lone Star: Join diamonds into rows. When all of the rows are finished, join rows to complete blocks. You can make all eight first rows, then all eight second rows, and so on. Alternatively, you can make only enough units for one block at a time to keep it more interesting, if desired. In that case, join the first two diamonds of the first row for just one block. Then join the first two diamonds of the second row, the third row, and so on. Add the third diamond to each row. Proceed in this manner until all rows of one block are complete. Join rows in pairs, then join pairs and pairs of pairs as needed to finish the block.

AT A GLANCE: QUICK SCISSOR CUTTING & MACHINE PIECING

Sort the fabrics into two piles, one for A-grain diamonds and one for B-grain diamonds. You'll be placing the fabrics face up when cutting A-grain diamonds and face down when cutting B-grain diamonds. (See page 60 for more about grain lines.)

Layer four to six A-grain fabrics face up. Press. Hold (or pin) the paper pattern in place with the grain arrow parallel to the selvedge and the side that you marked with an "A" facing up. Cut around the pattern (seam allowances are included) without marking.

Layer four to six B-grain fabrics face down. Press. Hold (or pin) the paper pattern in place with the grain arrow parallel to the selvedge and the side that you marked "B" face down just as the fabric is. (The A side with the grain arrow is face up.) Cut around the pattern through all of the fabric layers.

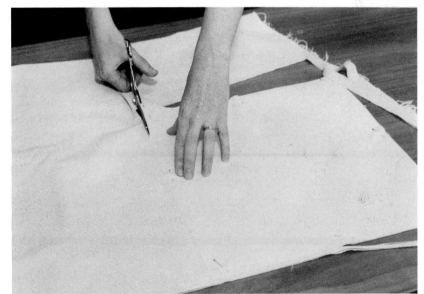

Cut background squares and triangles in a similar fashion. You can fold this fabric into four layers for speed. You may want to pin these large patterns in place before you cut the patches.

Arrange the diamond patches into a star point, stacking them eight deep. Spread the diamonds into rows.

All of the diamonds in the top layer are for one star point. Join the diamonds for one row of one star point. Repeat for the same row of the other star points. Continue in this fashion until you have made all of the rows and stacked them as shown.

All of the rows in the top layer are for one star point. Join rows into a star point as shown. Repeat with the rows in other layers to make eight star points.

Join four star points to form a half star. Repeat. Press these last long seam allowances all clockwise, as shown. Join halves. Add squares and triangles (see page 73) to complete the Lone Star.

ROTARY CUTTING AND STRIP PIECING

Machine piecers who are especially anxious for quick results often enjoy strip piecing. This method requires some special tools, but if you enjoy speedy techniques, you'll get plenty of use from them in future projects. To strip piece a Lone Star as we describe, you'll need a rotary cutter, mat, and a QuickStar© strip template. I found the usual strip piecing method and ordinary cutting rulers to be inconvenient for Lone Stars, so I designed a tool, the QuickStar, especially for Lone Stars. This tool is versatile enough to use for any Lone Star coloring having at least four star points alike. It eliminates measuring; you won't even have to measure the strip length. It is angled at the ends to save fabric and establish the line for cutting panels into rows. And the tips are trimmed to align strips perfectly for stitching.

Mapping Your Strategy. Looking at your colored quilt plan, isolate a single star point. You will need a strip to match the color of every diamond in the star point. You will join into a panel one strip for each diamond in a row. You will be making as many types of panels as there are rows of diamonds in the star point. Then you will cut the panels into strips, each strip being a row in the star point. All of the rows that you cut from one panel will be alike. You will need eight rows of each kind to complete eight star points for a Lone Star quilt. Each strip yields four rows. So for a standard Lone Star you will need two strips to match each diamond in a star point. Broken Stars and other variations can also be made using this strip method; however the number of strips needed may vary. Just remember that each strip makes four diamonds.

Planning Grain Lines. For strip piecing, ordinarily one cuts all strips on the lengthwise or crosswise grain. In a Lone Star quilt, this means that you will be joining bias to bias for the entire length of the seam between rows of diamonds. This requires a little extra care, but it is a viable way of constructing a Lone Star.

If you prefer to sew bias to straight for all seams, you can cut straight and bias strips alternately. Use the same plan of numbering rings described in the grain-line tips on page 60 for the scissor method. Cut all strips for diamonds in odd-numbered rings on the straight grain and all strips for diamonds in even-numbered rings on the bias. When you are joining strips, you will be sewing straight to bias. In order to avoid stretching the bias strip, you will want to be sure to use the QuickStar tool because it is important to cut strips precisely the same length and to cut both ends off at an angle to help you stagger the strips properly. You will also want to pin the strips before stitching. Lay the bias strip flat on the table with the straight strip face down over it when you pin for a perfectly smooth seam.

Cutting the Strips. Press fabrics, and layer four to six of them face up on the cutting mat. Be careful to align the grain of each piece. Using a rotary cutter and the QuickStar tool, trim off the selvedges. Use the markings on the tool to cut the strips.

Joining the Strips. Sew strips into panels. The sequence of fabrics should match that of the diamonds in the row. The angled ends will allow you to stagger the strips perfectly. It is not necessary to pin strips together unless some are cut on the bias. Simply hold the ends and stitch. Make a panel for each row in the star point. Each panel makes four identical rows. To have enough rows for eight matching star points, make two panels of each type needed.

Cutting the Panels into Rows. Press the seam allowances to one side. Press them all up in one panel and all down in the next panel. Use the

QuickStar tool to cut the panel into rows, using the same cutting guide markings that you used before. The tool has about ¼" extra length so you can trim off a slight amount on the panel ends for a crisp edge on each row.

If you like, you can trim off points at both ends of each row, using the end of the tool as a guide (turn the tool face down). This makes it easier to align rows properly for perfectly matched joints.

Joining Rows. Arrange the rows, in order, to form a star point. You can stack the identical rows and lay out eight star points at once, if you like. Join the rows and complete the quilt top just as you would for regular machine piecing.

AT A GLANCE: ROTARY CUTTING & STRIP PIECING

Layer four to six A-grain fabrics, face up, on a cutting mat. Cut straight-grain strips using the QuickStar tool and a rotary cutter. It is not necessary to measure strip lengths. Just cut around the tool. The ends are angled to help you align strips for stitching.

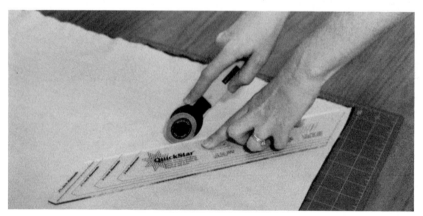

Layer four to six B-grain fabrics face up. Cut bias strips, aligning one short end of the QuickStar tool parallel to the selvedge.

Arrange strips in rows for one panel. Repeat for each type of panel. Stack strips for identical panels (usually you will be stacking strips two deep, as there are two panels of each type).

Pin the first two strips together, laying the bias strip flat on the table to keep it from stretching. Align the ends of the two strips. The straight-grain strip will not stretch; match the bias strip to it.

Stitch the strips together to make a panel, keeping the bias strip on the bottom. Make the correct number of panels of each type (usually two each, but it depends on the quilt design).

Make all of the panels needed. (This quilt requires five different panels as shown, with two of each type.) Press.

Cut the panels into strips (each one a row) using the Quick-Star tool and rotary cutter again. Cut across the seam lines, parallel to the edge.

The QuickStar tool was designed to make strips about $1/4"$ longer than necessary. This allows you to straighten the ends of the panel for clean, true strips.

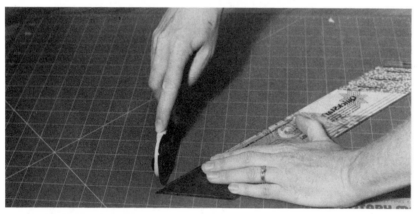

Turn the QuickStar tool face down and align it with the cut strip. Trim the tips of the strip to match the corners of the tool. This will help you align the rows for stitching later.

Arrange the strips for a star point, stacking all strips of a type. Complete the star as shown in the last two steps on page 64.

SPECIAL PIECING TIPS

This chapter provides explanations of some of the finer points of piecing. If you are already familiar with a technique such as chain piecing, feel free to skip that section. Don't miss the information on pages 71-74, though. These last five sections apply specifically to Lone Star quilts, and I think you'll find the material especially helpful. Over the years I've made a lot of Lone Star quilts, and I've learned a great deal about the easiest ways of doing things. I'd like to help you learn from my mistakes so you won't have to make your own. On these pages, I share the expertise I've gained making these quilts so that you can enjoy success with your very first Lone Star project.

PREPARATION

Test fabric to determine whether it is colorfast by hand rinsing one piece at a time in warm water. If the water runs clear, it is safe to wash several fabrics together in the washing machine. Machine wash and tumble dry. Smooth the wrinkles promptly.

THE NEED FOR ACCURACY

I cannot emphasize enough the need for accuracy in cutting and sewing. There is nothing difficult about making a Lone Star, but for your quilt to be one that will make you proud, you'll need to take some care. My best advice for precise seams is to double-check your seam gauge. Carefully trace a pattern from the book onto paper. Include seam lines as well as cutting lines, and cut out on the marked outer lines. Position the paper pattern as if you were going to sew, inserting the sewing machine needle into the marked seam line. Take a few stitches to be sure your paper is properly positioned. The cut edge of the pattern should be even with your seam gauge. You may be surprised to find that the seam allowance guide you have been using is not perfectly accurate. Adjust your needle position or add a properly positioned tape guide to make perfect seams.

MACHINE STITCHING GAUGE

For machine sewing, you will be stitching from edge to edge of the patch, backtacking at each end. There will be no marked line to follow; instead, stitch precisely 1/4" from the cut edge of the patch. Use the 1/4" guide on the throat plate of your machine or stick a piece of masking tape on the throatplate 1/4" from the needle. Run the edge of the patch along the guide for precise 1/4" seams.

Save thread and avoid tangles by chaining the units together. Seam two patches together, backtacking at both ends. Do not lift the presser foot. Do not cut the thread. Simply stop the machine, get the next two patches ready, slip them under the edge of the presser foot, and continue stitching. You may stitch through thin air for a couple of stitches, but do not overlap one unit and the next. Units will be connected by a chain of thread. Snip these threads to separate the units.

CHAIN PIECING

Good pressing can make the difference between a so-so quilt and a standout. Too much pressing can stretch bias edges and leave shiny marks on the fabric; too little can leave your quilt rumpled and possibly riddled with small tucks and folds.

PRESSING

The most important pressing is the pressing you give the fabric before you cut it into patches. Leave the fabric damp after prewashing and iron it dry and free of wrinkles. After the fabric is cut, you won't have another opportunity for a really good ironing, so take the trouble to do it now.

Proper pressing of the seam allowances as you piece the quilt can make the piecing and quilting easier and more enjoyable, and it can make your quilt sturdier and more attractive, as well.

Seam allowances in patchwork are best pressed to one side. This makes the quilt a little bulkier in places than it would be if you pressed the seams open, but pressing seams open allows the batting to seep out between the stitches. This seepage is impossible with seams pressed to one side.

If you plan ahead, you can press the seam allowances out of the way in areas where you will be quilting right next to the seam lines. This way, you can avoid quilting through extra layers. Your stitches will be smaller and more even, and the quilting will proceed more quickly and easily if you have pressed with the quilting in mind.

Pressing properly can also help you match the joints between diamonds in neighboring star points. By pressing seam allowances in opposite directions in adjacent rows of patches, you can reduce bulk in the seams as well as create a ridge that guides you in matching the joint perfectly.

When your quilt top is complete, you will want to give it a good pressing with the iron once again. Press from the back side first, approaching each seam from the side of the stitching line without the seam allowance. The motion is minimal, mainly just lifting and lowering the iron without sliding it around much. After pressing the back, turn over the quilt top and press it from the front.

FINGER-PRESSING

Actually, I find finger-pressing preferable to pressing with an iron during the quilt piecing. With finger-pressing (running your thumbnail along the fold of the seam line to train it into place), there is less danger of stretching bias edges, and the seam can be made to lie flatter, with less risk of stitching a small fold into your quilt.

LONE STAR PRESSING

The best way to press seams in a Lone Star is as follows: As you join diamonds to make a row, finger-press these short seams all to the right in one row and to the left in the next row. Then, when you join rows, the seam allowances won't bulge with all the layers in one place. After joining the rows to make a star point, all of the long seams remain free to be finger-pressed in the proper direction to oppose the seams in the adjoining star point.

After joining the four star points to make a half star, press the long seams between star points clockwise in each half, as shown in the last photo on page 64. Then, when you join halves, all the seams will oppose each other to help you match the joints and the center of the quilt.

Unless it will interfere with your quilting plans, seam allowances joining the background squares and triangles with the diamond star points should be pressed away from the star points. This avoids awkward and unnecessary bulk at the tips of the stars.

As you join two star points, the seams of one will have been stitched down already, and the seams of the other will remain free. Turn the free seam in the opposite direction from the stitched-down seam. Hold the neighboring patches at the joint. Keeping the cut edges of the two patches aligned, grip the patches between your thumb and forefinger and slide their seam allowances together. The seam allowances will form a ridge, and the two patches will not slip past the joint. When the patches are positioned properly, stick a pin at an angle to anchor both seam allowances. Repeat at each joint along the length of the seam, and stitch.

OPPOSING SEAMS

When joining rows to make star points, don't just pin and stitch. The matching is a little tricky here. To make perfect joints, set the sewing machine on a long (gathering) stitch. Pin, then machine baste each joint with four or five stitches in a contrasting thread color. Don't backstitch, and don't stitch the whole length of the seam. Just stitch over the joints. Check each joint. Pull out stitches of the poor joints and adjust them. When they are all perfect, readjust the machine to a normal stitch length and matching thread color. Stitch the whole length of the seam, right over your machine basting. Pull out the basting stitches carefully so that you won't break the permanent stitches.

QUICK-BASTING JOINTS

INSERTING BACKGROUND SQUARES AND TRIANGLES

When you join the star points, begin the line of stitching exactly at the start of the seam line at the corner to be set in. Stitch forward a couple of stitches, then backstitch, being careful to take the same number of stitches so that you neither overshoot nor undershoot your original starting point. Stitch forward to the opposite end of the seam. (You can stitch all the way to the cut edge of the patches except where you will be setting in the squares and triangles.) Turn the unit wrong side up. Align the edge of the square or triangle with the edge of one star point, with right sides together and the star point on top so that you can see the last seam line. The seam allowance joining the two star points should be pushed out of the way. Pin and stitch, starting your stitching line exactly at the start of the last seam. Be sure to backtack. You can stitch all the way to the cut edge at the other end of the star point. See the photograph below. Turn the unit over so that the background patch is on top. Pin and stitch the background patch to the adjacent star point. Again start stitching exactly where the last seam line began and push the seam allowances aside.

PERFECTING THE CENTER JOINT

The most important ingredient for a successful star center is accuracy in cutting and sewing. If you have cut patches with care, stitched with precise $1/4$" seams, and finger-pressed to avoid stretching bias edges, you should have no trouble achieving a perfectly flat, pucker-free center joint with seams matched precisely on all eight diamonds. There are a few tricks that will help, however, regardless of the sewing method you are using.

Machine Method. As you join the eight star points to make two half-stars, finger crease these long seams all the same way. For example, press toward the left after taking each seam. Then, when you join halves, the seams for the two halves will oppose perfectly. The bulk will be distributed evenly, and the joints will be easy to match because of the ridges formed by the opposing seams.

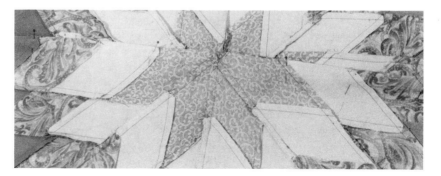

Hand Sewing Method. If you are hand sewing, your seam allowances will not have to be pressed either way before you finish the joint. If you stitch only to the end of the seam line and pass the needle to the other side of the allowance rather than catching the allowance in your stitching, you can use this trick to accomplish the flattest possible center joint: Once the stitching is complete, press the seam allowances all clockwise. Press down on the seam allowances at the center, and a star-shaped swirl will form there naturally.

Combination Method. Personally, I am more accurate on the sewing machine than I am sewing by hand. I get my best center joints by machine stitching. However, if you are machine stitching for speed but you are more comfortable with hand sewing when accuracy counts, try this: When you join star points to make a half star and when you join the halves to complete the star, stitch toward the center from the opposite end of the seam. Stitch just past the seam line that joins the center diamond to the second diamond. Leave the last couple of inches of each seam free. Mark seam lines and stitch these last few inches across the center by hand, pressing and swirling the seam allowances as described above.

Pressing the Joint. The center joint will be thick with all of the seam allowances that meet there. You'll need to take special care in pressing. You can easily scorch or put a shine on the high spot if you aren't careful. It is better not to press this joint from the top side of the quilt. The fabric will be forced into a mound over the seam allowances if you press from the top side. Instead, press only from the back. The joint will be flat against the ironing board, which will help keep the joint smooth. You won't risk shiny high spots on the quilt front this way, either. A pressing cloth may be used if you need to press from the front side.

Quilting the Joint. Finally, you'll need to use a little trick to keep your center flat after the quilting is done. Outline quilting each diamond $1/4"$ from the seam lines leaves a $3/4"$ area at the center of the star between quilting stitches. This will puff up and make a mountain out of even the smoothest of joints. You can remedy this by passing your needle into the seam line at the center and taking a couple of stitches through top and batting only before continuing the outline quilting. The stitches will flatten the center, and they will sink into the seam line where they won't show at all.

LONE STAR CHARTS

USEFULNESS OF THE CHARTS TO THOSE MAKING QUILTS FROM PATTERNS

This chapter provides easy-to-use charts to tell you dimensions and yardage requirements for dozens of Lone Star variations. Of course, if you will be making a Lone Star from one of the complete patterns given in the book, the figuring has been done you. You can feel free to skip over this chapter. However, if you feel moved to make any changes in a pattern, such as altering the color sequence to use five fabrics instead of ten, you'll be pleased to know how the charts can help you adjust the yardage figures. Also, if you plan to use the rotary cutting and strip-piecing method, you'll want to know how the yardage requirements might differ for this method.

It is really very easy to use the charts, so even a beginner can feel confident enough to make any pattern changes she desires. Each chart is preceded by a simple explanation of how and when to use it, plus an example. You might want to skim over the how's and when's just to know what kind of helps are available in case you should want to use them at some point.

USEFULNESS OF THE CHARTS TO THOSE DESIGNING ORIGINAL QUILTS OR VARIATIONS

If you are planning an original design, you will find this chapter invaluable. It takes the math completely out of the quilt-planning process. You can have the pleasure of being a creative designer without having to be a wizard at math. You can "write" your own pattern simply by looking up the answers in the charts. You can select any arrangement or border motif shown in the book. You can change the quilt size, the number or size of diamonds, or improvise on the color sequence. You can mix large and small diamonds. And you'll find all of the dimensions and yardages you need, at a glance. You'll even find full-size diamond patterns in a variety of sizes on page 85.

THE SIZE OF STAR POINT CHART

When to Use This Chart. You'll want to use the chart on the next page to figure out dimensions for background patches in your original design or variation. Background squares and triangles match the star point in dimensions. Kite-shaped background patches, such as those in the Radiant Star quilt on page 53, and rectangular patches, such as those in Unfolding Star on page 55, each have two sides the same length as the star point, as well. For this reason, you will want to use this chart to help you draft the large patterns needed to complete your original quilt.

How to Use This Chart. The sizes of diamonds (the side measurement not including seam allowances) are listed at the left side of the chart. The numbers of diamonds per row in the star point are listed across the top of the chart. Where the row for the desired diamond size meets the column for the correct number of diamonds per row you will find the finished measurement of one side of the star point.

Example. You want to make a quilt in a Stars and Cubes arrangement (page 13) using two-inch diamonds and seven diamonds per row. What size background patches do you need? On the Size of Star Points chart, find the row for two-inch diamonds. Follow it to the right to the column for seven diamonds per row. Your star point must measure 14" (not including seam allowances). Your background squares and triangles also measure 14" (not including seam allowances). The rectangular patch measures 14" on two sides. The other two sides are twice as long as a star point, or 28".

SIZE OF STAR POINT

♦ Size	NUMBER OF DIAMONDS PER ROW												
	3	4	5	6	7	8	9	10	11	12	13	14	15
1¹/₂"	4¹/₂	6	7¹/₂	9	10¹/₂	12	13¹/₂	15	16¹/₂	18	19¹/₂	21	22¹/₂
1³/₄"	5¹/₄	7	8³/₄	10¹/₂	12¹/₄	14	15³/₄	17¹/₂	19¹/₄	21	22³/₄	24¹/₂	26¹/₅
2"	6	8	10	12	14	16	18	20	22	24	26	28	30
2¹/₄"	6³/₄	9	11¹/₄	13¹/₂	15³/₄	18	20¹/₄	22¹/₂	24³/₄	27	29¹/₄	31¹/₂	–
2¹/₂"	7¹/₂	10	12¹/₂	15	17¹/₂	20	22¹/₂	25	27¹/₂	30	–	–	–
2³/₄"	8¹/₄	11	13³/₄	16¹/₂	19¹/₄	22	24³/₄	27¹/₂	30¹/₄	–	–	–	–
3"	9	12	15	18	21	24	27	30	–	–	–	–	–

INDICATES FINISHED MEASUREMENT ALONG ONE SIDE OF STAR POINT, IN INCHES.

THE QUILT DIMENSIONS CHARTS

When to Use These Charts. Use these charts to help you plan the size of diamond and number of diamonds per row suitable for your desired quilt size and arrangement. Or use them to determine the dimensions of a quilt when you know what size diamond and what arrangement you want.

How to Use These Charts. There are nine charts in this section. They list quilt sizes in inches for quilts of various arrangements. Select the chart for your chosen arrangement. (The names correspond to the diagrams on pages 11-17.) Diamond patch sizes from 1¹/₂" to 3" are listed on the left of each chart. (The number is the measurement along the seam line of one edge of the diamond.) The numbers of diamonds per row in the star point are listed across the top of the chart. Follow the row for your selected diamond size over to the column for the correct number of diamonds per row. Where the two cross, you will find the quilt size (before borders).

If you know the quilt size and diamond size, you can use these charts to find out how many diamonds per row you will need. Simply find the row for your diamond size. Follow it to the right to the correct quilt size. Now follow this column to the top of the chart for the number of diamonds per row.

Examples. 1) You want to make a Lone Star with 2¹/₂" diamonds and ten diamonds per row. Use the Lone Star chart below. Find 2¹/₂" on the left of the chart. Follow that row to the right to the column headed 10. Your quilt size is 85³/₈".

2) You want to make a Broken Star quilt of about 100" using 2¹/₂" diamonds. Use the chart at the top of page 77. Find 2¹/₂" on the left. Follow that row to the right to the quilt size closest to 100". In this case, the number is 102³/₈". Follow that column to the top of the chart to see that you will need six diamonds per row to make the quilt in your desired size.

QUILT DIMENSIONS – LONE STAR AND FLYING STAR

♦ Size	NUMBER OF DIAMONDS PER ROW												
	3	4	5	6	7	8	9	10	11	12	13	14	15
1¹/₂"	15³/₈	20¹/₂	25⁵/₈	30³/₄	35⁷/₈	41	46¹/₈	51¹/₄	56³/₈	61¹/₂	66⁵/₈	71³/₄	76⁷/₈
1³/₄"	17⁷/₈	23⁷/₈	29⁷/₈	35⁷/₈	41⁷/₈	47³/₄	53³/₄	59³/₄	65³/₄	71³/₄	77⁵/₈	83⁵/₈	89⁵/₈
2"	20¹/₂	27³/₈	34¹/₈	41	47³/₄	54⁵/₈	61¹/₂	68¹/₄	75¹/₈	82	88³/₄	95⁵/₈	102³/₈
2¹/₄"	23	30³/₄	38³/₈	46¹/₈	53³/₄	61¹/₂	69¹/₈	76⁷/₈	84¹/₂	92¹/₈	99⁷/₈	107¹/₂	–
2¹/₂"	25⁵/₈	34¹/₈	42⁵/₈	51¹/₄	59³/₄	68¹/₄	76⁷/₈	85³/₈	93⁷/₈	102³/₈	–	–	–
2³/₄"	28¹/₈	37¹/₂	47	56³/₈	65³/₄	75¹/₈	84¹/₂	93⁷/₈	103¹/₄	–	–	–	–
3"	30³/₄	41	51¹/₄	61¹/₂	71³/₄	82	92¹/₈	102³/₈	–	–	–	–	–

INDICATES FINISHED MEASUREMENT OF QUILT BEFORE BORDERS, IN INCHES.

QUILT DIMENSIONS – BROKEN STAR, STARS & CUBES, UNFOLDING STAR, MARINER'S STAR, POINSETTIA, AND MOTHER'S PRIDE

◆ Size	NUMBER OF DIAMONDS PER ROW							
	3	4	5	6	7	8	9	10
1½"	30¾	41	51¼	61½	71¾	82	92⅛	102⅜
1¾"	35⅞	47¾	59¾	71¾	83⅝	95⅝	107½	–
2"	41	54⅝	68¼	82	95⅝	109¼	–	–
2¼"	46⅛	61½	76⅞	92⅛	107½	–	–	–
2½"	51¼	68¼	85⅜	102⅜	–	–	–	–
2¾"	56⅜	75⅛	93⅞	–	–	–	–	–
3"	61½	82	102½	–	–	–	–	–

INDICATES FINISHED MEASUREMENT OF QUILT BEFORE BORDERS, IN INCHES.

QUILT DIMENSIONS – RADIANT STAR

◆ Size	NUMBER OF DIAMONDS PER ROW										
	3	4	5	6	7	8	9	10	11	12	13
1½"	24⅜	32½	40⅝	48¾	56⅞	65	73⅛	81¼	89⅜	97½	105⅝
1¾"	28⅜	37⅞	47⅜	56⅞	66⅜	75¾	85¼	94¾	104¼	–	–
2"	32½	43⅜	54⅛	65	75¾	86⅝	97½	108¼	–	–	–
2¼"	36½	48¾	60⅞	73⅛	85¼	97½	–	–	–	–	–
2½"	40⅝	54⅛	67⅝	81¼	94¾	108¼	–	–	–	–	–
2¾"	44⅝	59½	74½	89⅜	104¼	–	–	–	–	–	–
3"	48¾	65	81¼	97½	–	–	–	–	–	–	–

INDICATES FINISHED MEASUREMENT OF QUILT BEFORE BORDERS, IN INCHES.

QUILT DIMENSIONS – EARTH & STARS, SPRING STAR, ROLLING STAR, ECHOING STAR, LOVE-IN-A-MIST, AND WREATHED STAR

◆ Size	NUMBER OF DIAMONDS PER ROW											
	3	4	5	6	7	8	9	10	11	12	13	14
1½"	21¾	29	36¼	43½	50¾	58	65⅛	72⅜	79⅝	86⅞	94⅛	101⅜
1¾"	25⅜	33¾	42¼	50¾	59⅛	67⅝	76	84½	93	101⅜	–	–
2"	29	38⅝	48¼	58	67⅝	77¼	86⅞	95⅝	106¼	–	–	–
2¼"	32⅝	43½	54⅜	65⅛	76	86⅞	97¾	108⅝	–	–	–	–
2½"	36¼	48¼	60⅜	72⅜	84½	96⅝	108⅝	–	–	–	–	–
2¾"	39⅞	53⅛	66⅜	79⅝	93	106¼	–	–	–	–	–	–
3"	43½	58	72⅜	86⅞	101⅜	–	–	–	–	–	–	–

INDICATES FINISHED MEASUREMENT OF QUILT BEFORE BORDERS, IN INCHES.

QUILT DIMENSIONS – FANCIFUL STAR

◆ Size	NUMBER OF DIAMONDS PER ROW										
	3	4	5	6	7	8	9	10	11	12	13
1½"	22¼	27¾	33¼	38⅞	44⅜	50	55½	61	66⅝	72⅛	77¾
1¾"	25⅞	32⅜	38⅞	45⅜	51¾	58¼	64¾	71¼	77¾	84⅛	90⅝
2"	29⅝	37	44⅜	51¾	59¼	66⅝	74	81⅜	88¾	96¼	103⅝
2¼"	33¼	41⅝	50	58¼	66⅝	74⅞	83¼	91⅝	99⅞	108¼	–
2½"	37	46¼	55½	64¾	74	83¼	92½	101¾	111	–	–
2¾"	40¾	50⅞	61	71¼	81⅜	91⅝	101¾	111⅞	–	–	–
3"	44⅜	55½	66⅝	77¾	88¾	99⅞	111	–	–	–	–

INDICATES FINISHED MEASUREMENT OF QUILT BEFORE BORDERS, IN INCHES.

QUILT DIMENSIONS – FLYING SWALLOWS AND GRAND STAR

◆ Size	NUMBER OF DIAMONDS PER ROW									
	3	4	5	6	7	8	9	10	11	12
1½"	37⅛	49½	61⅞	74⅛	86½	98⅞	111¼	–	–	–
1¾"	43¼	57⅝	72⅛	86½	101	115⅜	–	–	–	–
2"	49½	66	82⅜	98⅞	115⅜	–	–	–	–	–
2¼"	55⅝	74⅛	92¾	111¼	–	–	–	–	–	–
2½"	61⅞	82⅜	103	–	–	–	–	–	–	–
2¾"	68	90⅝	113⅜	–	–	–	–	–	–	–
3"	74⅛	98⅞	–	–	–	–	–	–	–	–

INDICATES FINISHED MEASUREMENT OF QUILT BEFORE BORDERS, IN INCHES.

QUILT DIMENSIONS – GEM STAR

◆ Size	NUMBER OF DIAMONDS PER ROW												
	3	4	5	6	7	8	9	10	11	12	13	14	15
1½"	16⅝	22¼	27¾	33¼	38⅞	44⅜	50	55½	61	66⅝	72⅛	77¾	83¼
1¾"	19⅜	25⅞	32⅜	38⅞	45⅜	51¾	58¼	64¾	71¼	77¾	84⅛	90⅝	97⅛
2"	22¼	29⅝	37	44⅜	51¾	59¼	66⅝	74	81⅜	88¾	96¼	103⅝	111
2¼"	25	33¼	41⅝	50	58¼	66⅝	74⅞	83¼	91⅝	99⅞	108¼	–	–
2½"	27¾	37	46¼	55½	64¾	74	83¼	92½	101¾	111	–	–	–
2¾"	30½	40¾	50⅞	61	71¼	81⅜	91⅝	101¾	111⅞	–	–	–	–
3"	33¼	44⅜	55½	66⅝	77¾	88¾	99⅞	111	–	–	–	–	–

INDICATES FINISHED MEASUREMENT OF QUILT BEFORE BORDERS, IN INCHES.

QUILT DIMENSIONS – STAR OF LOVE

◆ Size	YARDAGE											
	3	4	5	6	7	8	9	10	11	12	13	14
1½"	19⅞	26½	33⅛	39¾	46⅜	53	59⅝	66¼	72⅞	79½	86⅛	92¾
1¾"	23⅛	30⅞	38⅝	46⅜	54⅛	61¾	69½	77¼	85	92¾	100⅜	108⅛
2"	26½	35⅜	44⅛	53	61¾	70⅝	79½	88¼	97⅛	106	—	—
2¼"	29¾	39¾	49⅝	59⅝	69½	79½	89⅜	99⅜	109¼	—	—	—
2½"	33⅛	44⅛	55⅛	66¼	77¼	88¼	99⅜	110⅜	—	—	—	—
2¾"	36⅜	48½	60¾	72⅞	85	97⅛	109¼	—	—	—	—	—
3"	39¾	53	66¼	79½	92¾	106	—	—	—	—	—	—

INDICATES FINISHED MEASUREMENT OF QUILT BEFORE BORDERS, IN INCHES.

QUILT DIMENSIONS – COUNTRY ROSE STAR AND LANCASTER ROSE STAR

◆ Size	NUMBER OF DIAMONDS PER ROW										
	3	4	5	6	7	8	9	10	11	12	13
1½"	36	48	60	72	84	96	108	—	—	—	—
1¾"	42	56	70	84	98	—	—	—	—	—	—
2"	48	64	80	96	—	—	—	—	—	—	—
2¼"	54	72	90	108	—	—	—	—	—	—	—
2½"	60	80	100	—	—	—	—	—	—	—	—
2¾"	66	88	110	—	—	—	—	—	—	—	—
3"	72	96	—	—	—	—	—	—	—	—	—

INDICATES FINISHED MEASUREMENT OF QUILT BEFORE BORDERS, IN INCHES.

THE BORDER WIDTH CHARTS

When to Use These Charts. You may want to make a central star that fits the top of the bed with pieced borders to drop at the sides and bottom and to cover the pillow area. In order to plan a border in the appropriate width to achieve your desired drop and quilt size, simply use these charts.

How to Use These Charts. The charts on page 80 indicate the widths of pieced borders of various designs and sizes. At the left are diamond sizes from 1½" to 3". Across the top of each chart are various border designs. Find the proper diamond size at the left. Follow the row for this entry to the right to the column for the correct design. Where row and column meet, you will find the width of one border (in inches). For 9-diamond motifs, look up the border widths for single-diamond and 4-diamond motifs (using both charts), and add the widths together.

Example. You are making a Lone Star quilt with 2½" diamonds. You want a border that is eight or nine inches wide to drop down at the sides and foot of the bed and to cover the pillows. Look up 2½" at the left of the chart. Deciding that you want a single-diamond border motif, you select the first chart. Find the 2½" entry at the left. Follow it to the right to a number around eight or nine inches. In this case, it is the number 8½", in the far right column. Looking at the top of the chart, you will see the design that will give you the border width you desire.

BORDER WIDTHS, SINGLE-DIAMOND MOTIFS

Diamond Size	BORDER DESIGNS				
1½"	2¾	2½	2⅛	3⅝	5⅛
1¾"	3¼	3	2½	4¼	6
2"	3¾	3⅜	2⅞	4⅞	6⅞
2¼"	4⅛	3⅞	3⅛	5⅜	7⅝
2½"	4⅝	4¼	3½	6	8½
2¾"	5⅛	4¾	3⅞	6⅝	9⅜
3"	5½	5⅛	4¼	7¼	10¼

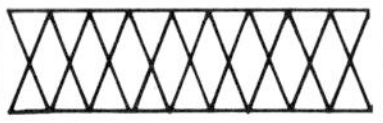

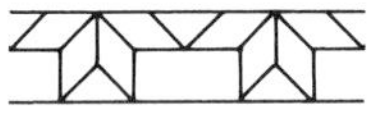

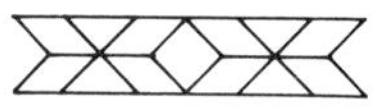

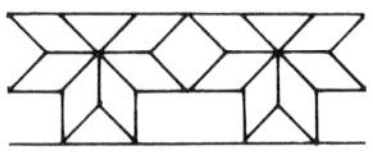

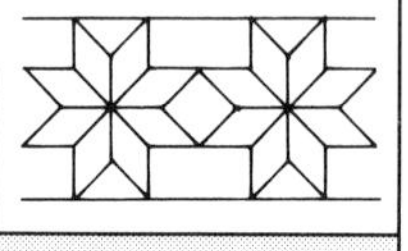

INDICATES WIDTH IN INCHES OF ONE PIECED BORDER STRIP.

BORDER WIDTHS, 4-DIAMOND MOTIFS

Diamond Size	BORDER DESIGNS				
1½"	5½	5⅛	4¼	7¼	10¼
1¾"	6½	6	5	8½	12
2"	7⅜	6⅞	5⅝	9⅝	13⅝
2¼"	8⅜	7⅝	6⅜	10⅞	15⅜
2½"	9¼	8½	7⅛	12⅛	17⅛
2¾"	10⅛	9⅜	7¾	13¼	18¾
3"	11⅛	10¼	8½	14½	20½

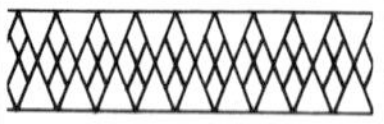

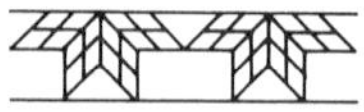

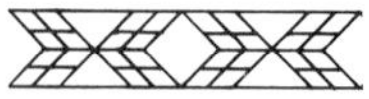

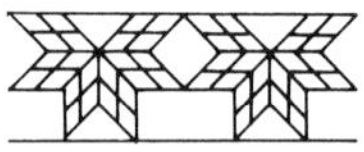

INDICATES WIDTH IN INCHES OF ONE PIECED BORDER STRIP.

YARDAGE CHARTS FOR DIAMONDS, SQUARES, AND TRIANGLES

When to Use These Charts. These charts are especially helpful, whether you are planning an original design or just changing the color sequence of a pattern in the book. Use them to find out how much fabric to buy or to find out if a piece of fabric you have will be large enough to cut the required patches.

How to Use These Charts. Yardage charts can be found on pages 81-83. When you have decided just which fabrics you will be using in your design and where each one is placed, simply count the number of diamonds, squares, and triangles needed of each fabric. Then look up the yardage for each fabric, one at a time, in the appropriate chart. If you will be cutting more than one shape from the same fabric (squares and triangles, for example), look up the yardages for each shape separately, and add the yardages together to find the total amount needed.

There are three yardage charts, one for diamonds, one for squares, and one for triangles. Yardages listed are based on 44" fabric width. The calculations allow for 2% shrinkage. The cutting layouts were planned with two sides of each diamond or square or with the long side of each triangle on the lengthwise grain of fabric. The yardage amounts are sufficient if you are careful to cut diamonds edge to edge. Buy a little extra fabric if you want to center a print in a special way or if you want a little extra fabric for your scrap collection or in case of a cutting error.

Yardages are listed across the top of the chart. Finished side measurements of patches are at the left. These are the measurements along the seam lines, not including seam allowances. For triangles, the measurement of one of the two short sides is used. Find the row at the left listing your patch size. Follow that row to the right to the column listing the correct number of patches needed. If your number is not listed, go to the next larger number. Follow the column up to the top of the chart to see the yardage required.

Example. Your design calls for 256 diamonds to be cut from one fabric. The diamonds measure 2$\frac{1}{4}$" (finished) along one side. Find the row for 2$\frac{1}{4}$" diamonds. Follow it to the right to the column listing 285. This is the nearest number greater than 256. Look at the top of the column. You will need 1$\frac{3}{8}$ yards of fabric to cut the 256 diamonds.

YARDAGE FOR DIAMONDS

Finished Size of Diamond	YARDAGE																	
	$\frac{1}{8}$	$\frac{1}{4}$	$\frac{3}{8}$	$\frac{1}{2}$	$\frac{5}{8}$	$\frac{3}{4}$	$\frac{7}{8}$	1	1$\frac{1}{8}$	1$\frac{1}{4}$	1$\frac{3}{8}$	1$\frac{1}{2}$	1$\frac{5}{8}$	1$\frac{3}{4}$	1$\frac{7}{8}$	2	2$\frac{1}{8}$
1$\frac{1}{2}$"	26	78	130	182	234	286	338	364	416	468	520	572	624	676	728	780	832
1$\frac{5}{8}$"	25	75	100	150	200	250	300	350	400	425	475	525	575	625	675	725	750
1$\frac{3}{4}$"	23	46	92	138	184	207	253	299	345	368	414	460	506	529	575	621	667
1$\frac{7}{8}$"	–	44	88	132	154	198	242	264	308	352	374	418	462	484	528	572	594
2"	–	42	84	105	147	168	210	252	273	315	336	378	420	441	483	504	546
2$\frac{1}{8}$"	–	40	60	100	120	160	200	220	260	280	320	340	380	400	440	460	500
2$\frac{1}{4}$"	–	38	57	95	114	152	171	209	228	247	285	304	342	361	399	418	456
2$\frac{3}{8}$"	–	38	57	76	114	133	171	190	209	247	266	304	323	361	380	399	437
2$\frac{1}{2}$"	–	36	54	72	108	126	144	180	198	216	252	270	288	324	342	378	396
2$\frac{5}{8}$"	–	17	51	68	85	119	136	153	187	204	221	238	272	289	306	340	357
2$\frac{3}{4}$"	–	17	51	68	85	102	136	153	170	187	221	238	255	272	306	323	340
2$\frac{7}{8}$"	–	16	32	64	80	96	112	144	160	176	192	208	240	256	272	288	304
3"	–	15	30	45	75	90	105	120	135	165	180	195	210	225	240	270	285
3$\frac{1}{8}$"	–	15	30	45	60	90	105	120	135	150	165	180	210	225	240	255	270
3$\frac{1}{4}$"	–	14	28	42	56	70	98	112	126	140	154	168	182	196	210	224	252
3$\frac{3}{8}$"	–	14	28	42	56	70	84	98	112	126	154	168	182	196	210	224	238
3$\frac{1}{2}$"	–	13	26	39	52	65	78	91	104	117	130	143	156	169	182	195	208
3$\frac{5}{8}$"	–	13	26	39	52	65	78	91	104	117	130	143	156	169	182	195	208
3$\frac{3}{4}$"	–	13	26	39	52	65	78	91	104	117	130	143	156	169	169	182	195
3$\frac{7}{8}$"	–	12	24	36	48	60	60	72	84	96	108	120	132	144	156	168	180
4"	–	12	24	36	36	48	60	72	84	96	108	120	132	144	156	168	180

INDICATES NUMBER OF PATCHES OF DESIGNATED SIZES THAT CAN BE CUT FROM VARIOUS YARDAGES.

YARDAGE FOR BACKGROUND SQUARES

Fin. Size of Square	YARDAGE															
	$1/4$	$3/8$	$1/2$	$5/8$	$3/4$	$7/8$	1	$1 1/8$	$1 1/4$	$1 3/8$	$1 1/2$	$1 5/8$	$1 3/4$	$1 7/8$	2	$2 1/8$
5½"	7	14	14	21	28	35	35	42	49	56	56	63	70	77	77	84
6"	6	12	12	18	24	24	30	36	36	42	48	48	54	60	60	66
6½"	6	6	12	18	18	24	30	30	36	36	42	48	48	54	60	60
7"	5	5	10	10	15	20	20	25	25	30	35	35	40	40	45	45
7½"	5	5	10	10	15	15	20	20	25	30	30	35	35	40	40	45
8"	4	4	8	8	12	12	16	16	20	20	24	24	28	28	32	32
8½"	–	4	4	8	8	12	12	16	16	20	20	24	24	28	28	32
9"	–	4	4	8	8	12	12	16	16	20	20	24	24	24	28	28
9½"	–	4	4	8	8	12	12	12	16	16	20	20	24	24	28	28
10"	–	4	4	8	8	8	12	12	16	16	20	20	20	24	24	28
10½"	–	3	3	6	6	6	9	9	12	12	12	15	15	18	18	18
11"	–	3	3	3	6	6	9	9	9	12	12	12	15	15	18	18
11½"	–	3	3	3	6	6	6	9	9	12	12	12	15	15	15	18
12"	–	3	3	3	6	6	6	9	9	9	12	12	12	15	15	15
12½"	–	3	3	3	6	6	6	9	9	9	12	12	12	15	15	15
13"	–	–	3	3	3	6	6	6	9	9	9	12	12	12	15	15
13½"	–	–	3	3	3	6	6	6	9	9	9	12	12	12	15	15
14"	–	–	2	2	2	4	4	4	6	6	6	6	8	8	8	10
14½"	–	–	2	2	2	4	4	4	4	6	6	6	8	8	8	8
15"	–	–	2	2	2	2	4	4	4	6	6	6	6	8	8	8
15½"	–	–	2	2	2	2	4	4	4	6	6	6	6	8	8	8
16"	–	–	2	2	2	2	4	4	4	4	6	6	6	8	8	8
16½"	–	–	2	2	2	2	4	4	4	4	6	6	6	6	8	8
17"	–	–	2	2	2	2	4	4	4	4	6	6	6	6	8	8
17½"	–	–	–	2	2	2	2	4	4	4	4	6	6	6	6	8
18"	–	–	–	2	2	2	2	4	4	4	4	6	6	6	6	8
18½"	–	–	–	2	2	2	2	4	4	4	4	6	6	6	6	6
19"	–	–	–	2	2	2	2	4	4	4	4	4	6	6	6	6
19½"	–	–	–	2	2	2	2	2	4	4	4	4	6	6	6	6
20"	–	–	–	2	2	2	2	2	4	4	4	4	6	6	6	6

INDICATES NUMBER OF PATCHES OF DESIGNATED SIZES THAT CAN BE CUT FROM VARIOUS YARDAGES.

YARDAGE FOR BACKGROUND TRIANGLES

Fin. Size of Triangle	YARDAGE														
	$3/8$	$1/2$	$5/8$	$3/4$	$7/8$	1	$1 1/8$	$1 1/4$	$1 3/8$	$1 1/2$	$1 5/8$	$1 3/4$	$1 7/8$	2	$2 1/8$
5$1/2$"	9	18	27	36	45	54	63	72	81	90	99	108	117	126	135
6"	8	16	24	32	40	48	56	64	64	72	80	88	96	104	112
6$1/2$"	8	16	24	32	32	40	48	56	64	72	72	80	88	96	104
7"	7	14	14	21	28	35	42	42	49	56	63	70	70	77	84
7$1/2$"	7	7	14	21	28	28	35	42	49	49	56	63	70	70	77
8"	6	6	12	18	18	24	30	36	36	42	48	48	54	60	60
8$1/2$"	–	6	12	12	18	24	24	30	36	36	42	48	48	54	60
9"	–	6	12	12	18	24	24	30	30	36	42	42	48	54	54
9$1/2$"	–	5	10	10	15	15	20	25	25	30	30	35	40	40	45
10"	–	5	5	10	15	15	20	20	25	25	30	35	35	40	40
10$1/2$"	–	5	5	10	10	15	15	20	25	25	30	30	35	35	40
11"	–	5	5	10	10	15	15	20	20	25	25	30	30	35	35
11$1/2$"	–	4	4	8	8	12	12	16	16	20	20	24	24	28	28
12"	–	–	4	4	8	8	12	12	16	16	20	20	24	24	28
12$1/2$"	–	–	4	4	8	8	12	12	16	16	20	20	20	24	24
13"	–	–	4	4	8	8	12	12	12	16	16	20	20	24	24
13$1/2$"	–	–	4	4	8	8	8	12	12	16	16	20	20	20	24
14"	–	–	3	3	3	6	6	9	9	12	12	12	15	15	18
14$1/2$"	–	–	3	3	3	6	6	9	9	9	12	12	15	15	15
15"	–	–	–	3	3	6	6	6	9	9	12	12	12	15	15
15$1/2$"	–	–	–	3	3	6	6	6	9	9	9	12	12	15	15
16"	–	–	–	3	3	3	6	6	9	9	9	12	12	12	15
16$1/2$"	–	–	–	3	3	3	6	6	6	9	9	12	12	12	15
17"	–	–	–	3	3	3	6	6	6	9	9	9	12	12	12
17$1/2$"	–	–	–	3	3	3	6	6	6	9	9	9	12	12	12
18"	–	–	–	–	3	3	3	6	6	6	9	9	9	12	12
18$1/2$"	–	–	–	–	3	3	3	6	6	6	9	9	9	12	12
19"	–	–	–	–	2	2	2	4	4	4	6	6	6	8	8
19$1/2$"	–	–	–	–	2	2	2	4	4	4	4	6	6	6	8
20"	–	–	–	–	2	2	2	2	4	4	4	6	6	6	8

INDICATES NUMBER OF PATCHES OF DESIGNATED SIZES THAT CAN BE CUT FROM VARIOUS YARDAGES.

When to Use These Charts. If you plan to make your Lone Star by the rotary cutting method with a QuickStar tool, you will want to make sure that you have sufficient yardage for this method. You may need a different amount of yardage to cut strips than you need to cut individual diamonds. You may have leftover fabric, as well, since you will need a certain length for one strip, though you may not need the full width of the fabric to cut the number of strips needed. There are two charts in this section, one for strips cut on the lengthwise grain and one for strips cut on the bias. Both of these types of strips yield diamonds with two edges on lengthwise grain and two edges on bias. We do not recommend *crosswise* grain because it is not as stable as the lengthwise grain and the print may not align well with the threads.

How to Use These Charts. Each strip you cut makes four diamonds. Diamond sizes are listed on the left of the charts below. Yardages are listed at the top. Select the chart for the grain you will be using for your strips. Find the row for your diamond size on the left. Follow this row to the right to the first number that is the same as or larger than the number of diamonds needed of one fabric. Where row and column meet, follow the column up to the top to see the required yardage. The number following the slash by the number of diamonds is the number of strips you can cut from the yardage listed (84/21 means that you can cut strips for up to 84 diamonds, which is to say that you can cut 21 strips).

Example. Your pattern calls for 56 diamonds of one fabric. Your strips will be cut on the lengthwise grain. Your diamond size is 2³/₄". Find 2³/₄" at the left of the first chart. Follow its row to the right to the first column listing 64. This is the nearest number greater than 56. Look at the top of the chart. You will need ¹/₂ yard of this fabric. You can cut up to 16 strips from ¹/₂ yard, although you will need only 14 strips to make the required number of diamonds. You'll have a little left to add to your scrap collection.

**THE STRIP
YARDAGE CHARTS**

YARDAGE FOR LENGTHWISE QUICKSTAR STRIPS

Size of Diamond	YARDAGE								
	³/₈	¹/₂	⁵/₈	³/₄	⁷/₈	1	1¹/₈	1¹/₄	1³/₈
2"	84/21	84/21	84/21	168/42	168/42	168/42	252/63	252/63	252/63
2¹/₄"	–	76/19	76/19	76/19	152/38	152/38	152/38	152/38	152/38
2¹/₂"	–	68/17	68/17	68/17	68/17	136/34	136/34	136/34	136/34
2³/₄"	–	64/16	64/16	64/16	64/16	128/32	128/32	128/32	128/32

INDICATES NUMBER OF DIAMONDS/NUMBER OF STRIPS THAT CAN BE CUT FROM VARIOUS YARDAGES.

YARDAGE FOR BIAS QUICKSTAR STRIPS

Size of Diamond	YARDAGE									
	¹/₄	³/₈	¹/₂	⁵/₈	³/₄	⁷/₈	1	1¹/₈	1¹/₄	1³/₈
2"	48/12	48/12	96/24	96/24	144/36	144/36	192/48	192/48	240/60	240/60
2¹/₄"	–	40/10	40/10	80/20	80/20	120/30	120/30	160/40	160/40	200/50
2¹/₂"	–	36/9	36/9	72/18	72/18	108/27	108/27	144/36	144/36	144/36
2³/₄"	–	32/8	32/8	64/16	64/16	64/16	96/24	96/24	128/32	128/32

INDICATES NUMBER OF DIAMONDS/NUMBER OF STRIPS THAT CAN BE CUT FROM VARIOUS YARDAGES.

PATTERNS

This section includes complete, full-size patterns for the quilts shown in color on pages 46-56. Each pattern lists yardage and cutting requirements. Diagrams illustrate piecing and quilting units. For more general help with quiltmaking procedures and Lone Star sewing tips, see pages 57-74.

Fabrics are numbered in the diagrams and yardage figures. This has been done to prevent confusion about exactly which fabric is meant. (Color names are so subjective.) The colors are numbered from the center out so that you can easily match the number to the fabric in the color photograph of the quilt. It's easy to make the quilts exactly as shown, or you can just as easily substitute other colors to make your own design variation.

The full-size pieced patterns include cutting lines (solid) and seam lines (dashed). Many also include dashed quilting lines. Arrows indicate straight of grain. Patterns for applique do not include turn-under allowances. Add $^3/_{16}$" around all sides of these patches "by eye" when you cut them from fabric. Where it was impossible to give the entire patch or quilting motif, a dotted line indicates the center line. A couple of patches were too large to show even half. You will need to add the listed number of inches between marks to complete the full-size patterns in these cases. A few of the patterns that were too large to fit on the page are diagrammed with the dimensions listed. You will need to add $^1/_4$" seam allowances all around on these patches. Please note that dimensions listed for border strips include $^1/_4$" seam allowances plus 2" extra length for insurance.

Additional diamond patterns, with dimensions, are given below so that you can use these patterns to create Lone Star variations of your own design without having to draft the templates. (Use the charts on pages 75-84 to keep the figuring to a minimum, as well.)

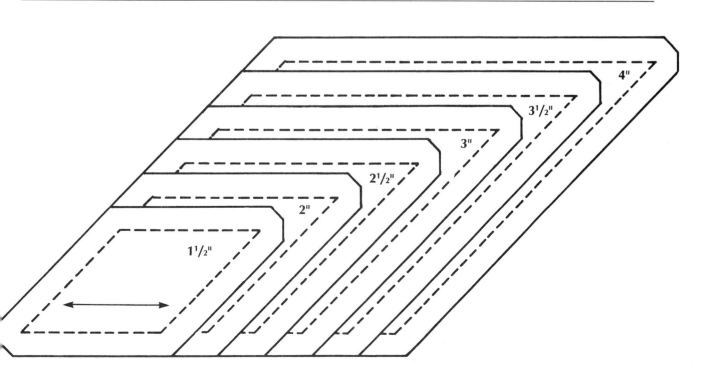

ECHOING STAR

Echoing Star condenses a Broken Star into a Rolling Star arrangement. The outer star points have fewer diamonds than the inner ones. This arrangement makes an attractive wall quilt. With the addition of four corner triangles to square off the octagon, this could be used as the center of a bed quilt. See the quilt in color on page 50.

HINT: In order for the outer diamond-shaped Z blocks to match the size of the inner star-point Y blocks, the Z blocks need to be enlarged slightly by the use of bordering strips. The A's are joined in fours to make Unit 1's. Then three Unit 1's are joined with four C's to make a diamond-shaped unit. An E and an Er are added and mitered where they meet to complete each Z block.

Yardage (44" fabric) & Cutting Requirements

Diamond Size: $2\frac{1}{2}$"
Quilt Size: $60\frac{3}{8}$" x $60\frac{3}{8}$"
$1\frac{1}{4}$ **yds. Fabric #1:** binding $1\frac{1}{2}$" x $6\frac{1}{4}$ yds., 64 A
$\frac{3}{8}$ **yd. Fabric #2:** 48 A
$\frac{5}{8}$ **yd. Fabric #3:** 40 A, 8 B, 8 Br
$1\frac{3}{8}$ **yds. Fabric #4:** 16 A, 8 D
$\frac{1}{2}$ **yd. Fabric #5:** 32 A, 8 E, 8 Er
$\frac{1}{2}$ **yd. Fabric #6:** 64 A
$\frac{1}{2}$ **yd. Fabric #7:** 32 C
Batting: $64\frac{1}{2}$" x $64\frac{1}{2}$"
Lining: $3\frac{3}{4}$ yds.

Referring to diagrams, make eight Y blocks and eight Z blocks.

Join four Y blocks to make a half star. Repeat. Join halves. Add D's and Z blocks as shown in the quilt diagram at right.

See the quilting figure on page 88. Add the heart to the tip of the motif, matching dots and fold lines. Trace the motif on half of a $12\frac{1}{2}$" square of paper folded diagonally. Trace the reverse of the motif on the other half. Mark this motif in each D patch, with the hearts at

the inner corners of the D's. Quilt as marked. Outline quilt the A, B, Br, C, and D patches $\frac{1}{4}$" from seam lines. Quilt "in the ditch" around E's and Er's. Bind to finish.

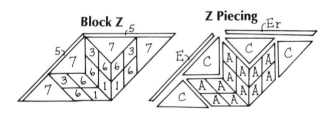

Block Z **Z Piecing**

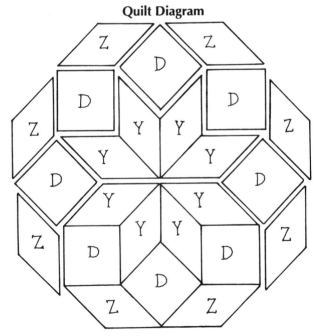

Quilt Diagram

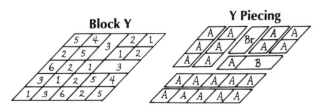

Block Y **Y Piecing**

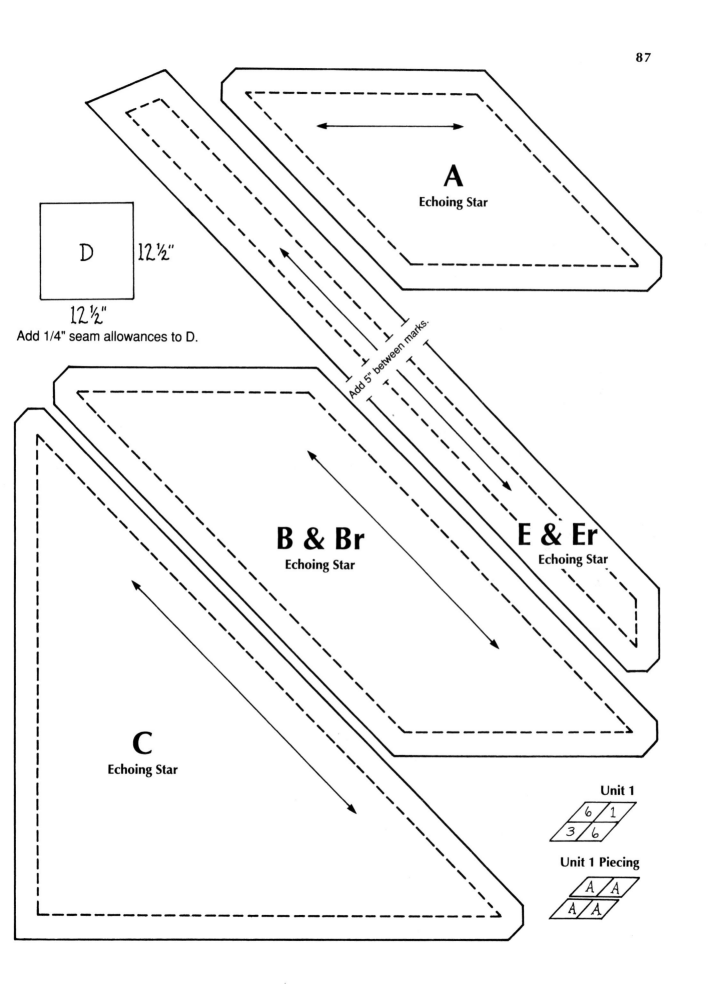

A
Echoing Star

D

12½"

12½"

Add 1/4" seam allowances to D.

Add 5" between marks.

B & Br
Echoing Star

E & Er
Echoing Star

C
Echoing Star

Unit 1

6	1
3	6

Unit 1 Piecing

A	A
A	A

88

Place on fold

Quilting for D

Place on fold

WREATHED STAR

Wreathed Star is a Lone Star variation in the Rolling Star arrangement. To square off the corners, pieced triangles were added. The piecing here ties together the diamond-shaped blocks around the outside of the quilt with a flourish. A color photo of this quilt is on page 46.

HINT: The central star's points are colored two ways, light and dark versions of the same basic color sequence. Fabrics just a step apart in value were chosen. This effect is more easily accomplished in a quilt of several colors than in a monochromatic quilt. That way, you don't have to find so many "just right" shades of only one color. The rings of color reverse at the widest ring and repeat.

Yardage (44" fabric) & Cutting Requirements

Diamond Size: 2"
Quilt Size: 58" x 58"
$1/4$ **yd. Fabric #1:** 40 A
$3/8$ **yd. Fabric #2:** 48 A
$1/4$ **yd. Fabric #3:** 24 A
$5/8$ **yd. Fabric #4:** 32 A, 8 E
$3/8$ **yd. Fabric #5:** 48 A
$1/4$ **yd. Fabric #6:** 24 A
$1/4$ **yd. Fabric #7:** 40 A
$3/8$ **yd. Fabric #8:** 48 A
$1^1/8$ **yds. Fabric #9:** binding $1^1/2$" x 7 yds., 88 A
$5/8$ **yd. Fabric #10:** 112 A
$1/4$ **yd. Fabric #11:** 24 A
$1/4$ **yd. Fabric #12:** 24 A
$1/4$ **yd. Fabric #13:** 24 A
$3/8$ **yd. Fabric #14:** 64 A
$1^3/8$ **yds. Fabric #15:** 8 B, 16 C, 4 D
Batting: 62" x 62"
Lining: $3^5/8$ yds.

Referring to block coloring and piecing diagrams, make four W blocks, four X blocks, eight Y blocks, and four Z blocks. Join blocks and B's as shown in the quilt diagram on page 91.

See the quilting figure on page 91. Trace the quarter-motif given in each quadrant of a 12" paper square folded in half lengthwise and in half again crosswise. Mark and quilt this complete motif in the B patches. Quilt as marked. Quilt "in the ditch" around all patches. Bind to finish.

Block W   **Block X**

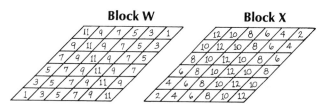

Block Y

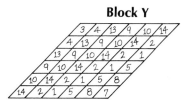

W, X & Y Piecing

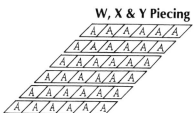

Block Z   **Z Piecing**

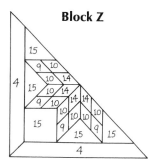
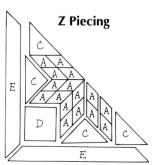

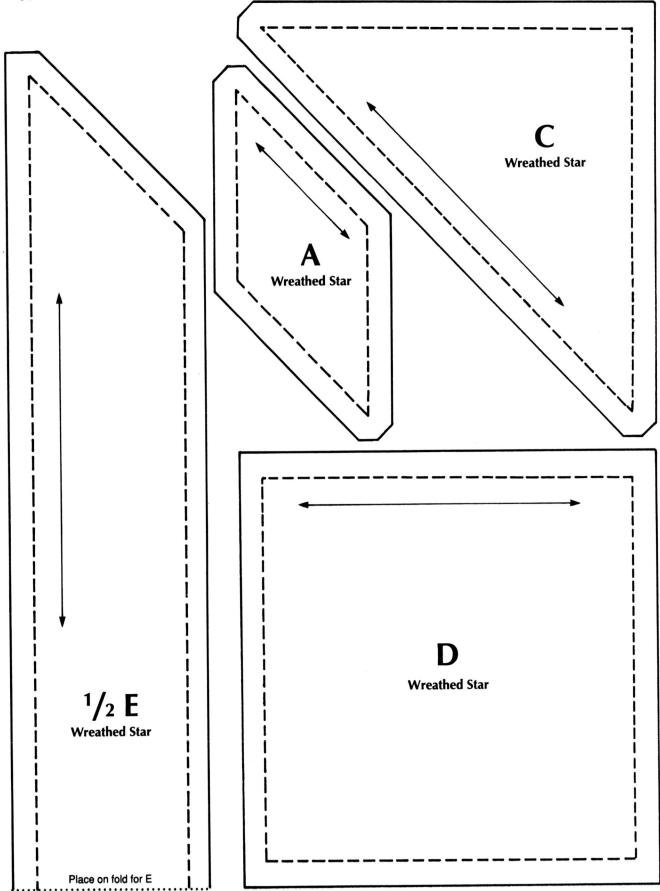

C
Wreathed Star

A
Wreathed Star

½ E
Wreathed Star

Place on fold for E

D
Wreathed Star

Quilting for B

Quilt Diagram

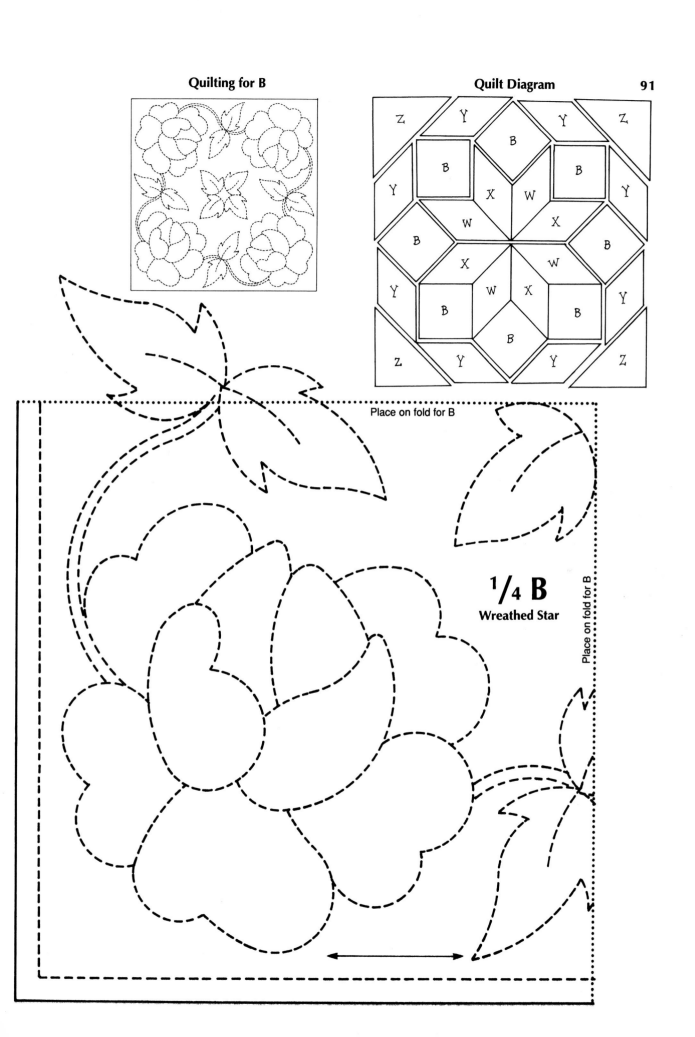

Place on fold for B

¹/₄ B
Wreathed Star

Place on fold for B

LANCASTER ROSE STAR

Lancaster Rose Star glows in radiant solid colors. The dark background provides an interesting contrast to the bright star points. A pretty floral motif is quilted in the background for a finishing touch. The quilt is shown in color on page 54.

HINT: Use ³/₄" masking tape to "mark" the quilting in the background (C) triangles. As you are ready to quilt a triangle, lay a strip of tape on the triangle with one edge along the base of the triangle. Quilt along both edges of the tape. Move the tape over ³/₄" so that its other edge is now aligned with the quilting stitches just completed. Quilt along the other edge of the tape. Continue in this fashion until all of the triangles are quilted in stripes, using fresh strips of tape as the old ones deteriorate.

Yardage (44" fabric) & Cutting Requirements

Diamond: 2¹/₂"
Quilt Size: 60" x 60"
1¹/₄ yds. Fabric #1: 8 A, 48 C
¹/₂ yd. Fabric #2: 64 A
⁵/₈ yd. Fabric #3: 96 A
2¹/₄ yds. Fabric #4: 64 A, 4 D, 4 Dr
¹/₄ yd. Fabric #5: 32 A
1¹/₄ yds. Fabric #6: binding 1¹/₂" x 7¹/₄ yds., 8 B
¹/₄ yd. Fabric #7: 24 A
Batting: 64" x 64"
Lining: 3³/₄ yds.

Referring to diagrams, make eight Y blocks and 24 Z blocks.

Join blocks, B's, C's, D's, and Dr's as shown in quilt diagram.

Mark the quilting motif given in B patches. (This is shown with solid lines because it is also used as the applique motif for the Country Rose Star pattern on pages 94-95.) Also use the B motif three times (leaving off one leaf at the end) in each D patch as shown in the figure on page 93. Reverse this three-bud motif for Dr patches. Quilt as marked. Quilt "in the ditch" around A's. Use masking tape to mark and quilt parallel lines ³/₄" apart in C patches. Bind to finish.

Piecing

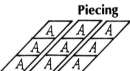

Block Y   **Block Z**

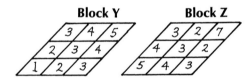

Quilt Diagram

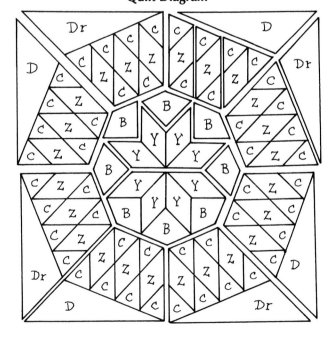

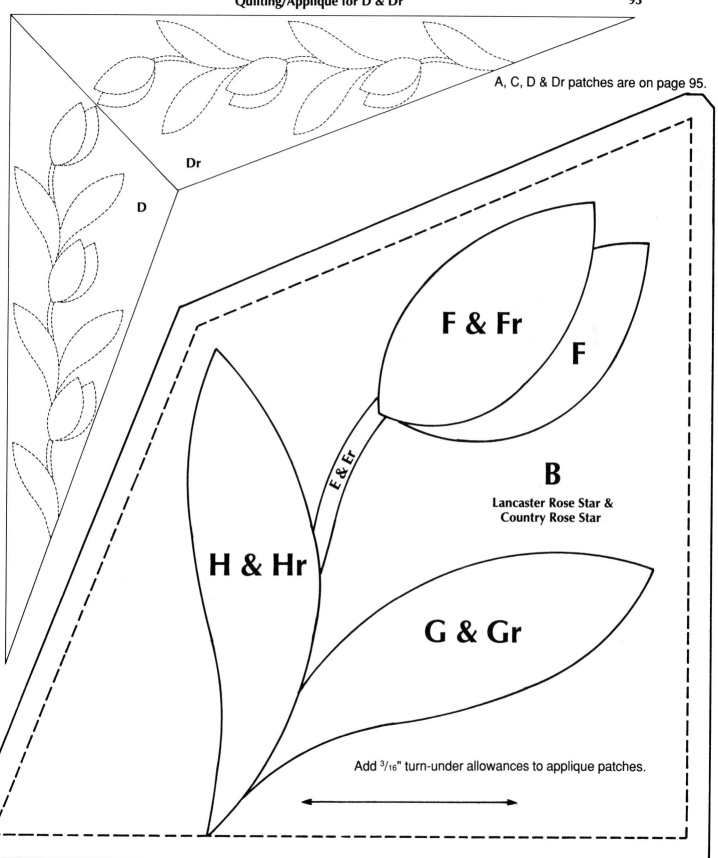

A, C, D & Dr patches are on page 95.

Dr

D

F & Fr

F

E & Er

B

**Lancaster Rose Star &
Country Rose Star**

H & Hr

G & Gr

Add ³/₁₆" turn-under allowances to applique patches.

COUNTRY ROSE STAR

Country Rose Star is the same basic pattern as the Lancaster Rose Star pattern on page 92. Here, colors are softer and prints replace the solids. The flower motif is appliqued in this version, whereas in the Lancaster Rose Star quilt it is quilted. See both quilts in color on page 54.

HINT: For invisible applique stitches, match the sewing thread to each patch rather than to the background fabric.

Yardage (44" fabric) & Cutting Requirements

Diamond Size: 2$\frac{1}{2}$"
Quilt Size: 60" x 60"
2 yds. Fabric #1: bias stripping $\frac{3}{4}$" x 2$\frac{1}{4}$ yds. for 32 E; 8 A, 48 C, 16 G, 8 Gr, 20 H, 12 Hr
$\frac{1}{4}$ yd. Fabric #2: 16 A
$\frac{5}{8}$ yd. Fabric #3: 96 A
1$\frac{5}{8}$ yds. Fabric #4: binding 1$\frac{1}{2}$" x 7$\frac{1}{4}$ yds., 88 A, 20 F, 12 Fr
$\frac{7}{8}$ yd. Fabric #5: 80 A, 20 F, 12 Fr
2$\frac{1}{4}$ yds. Fabric #6: 8 B, 4 D, 4 Dr
Batting: 64" x 64"
Lining: 3$\frac{3}{4}$ yds.

Referring to diagrams at right, make eight Y blocks and 24 Z blocks.

Turn under $\frac{3}{16}$" around edges of applique patches and baste. For bias stem strips, fold the $\frac{3}{4}$" bias stripping in half lengthwise with right sides out. Stitch $\frac{1}{8}$" from raw edges. Press so that the seam allowance is hidden under the strip as shown in Figure 1 on page 95. Cut into 32 pieces, each 2$\frac{1}{2}$" long, for stems.

Position a stem, then two leaves and two petals, on each B patch, and baste in place. Blindstitch. Similarly, applique three flowers (minus one G leaf) in each D patch, as shown in the figure on page 93. Applique three flowers reversed (minus one Gr leaf) in each Dr patch.

Join blocks, B's, C's, D's, and Dr's as shown in quilt diagram at right.

Mark the quilting motif given in C patches. Quilt as marked. Quilt "in the ditch" around appliques and A patches. Bind to finish.

Piecing

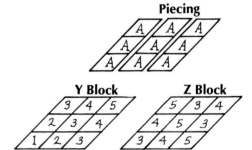

Y Block   **Z Block**

Quilt Diagram

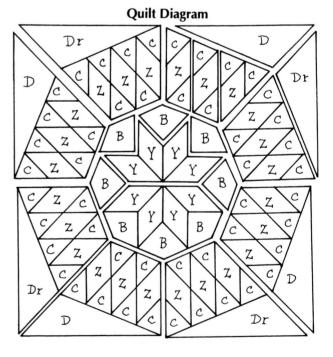

Add ¼" seam allowances to D & Dr.

B, E, F, G & H patches are on page 93.

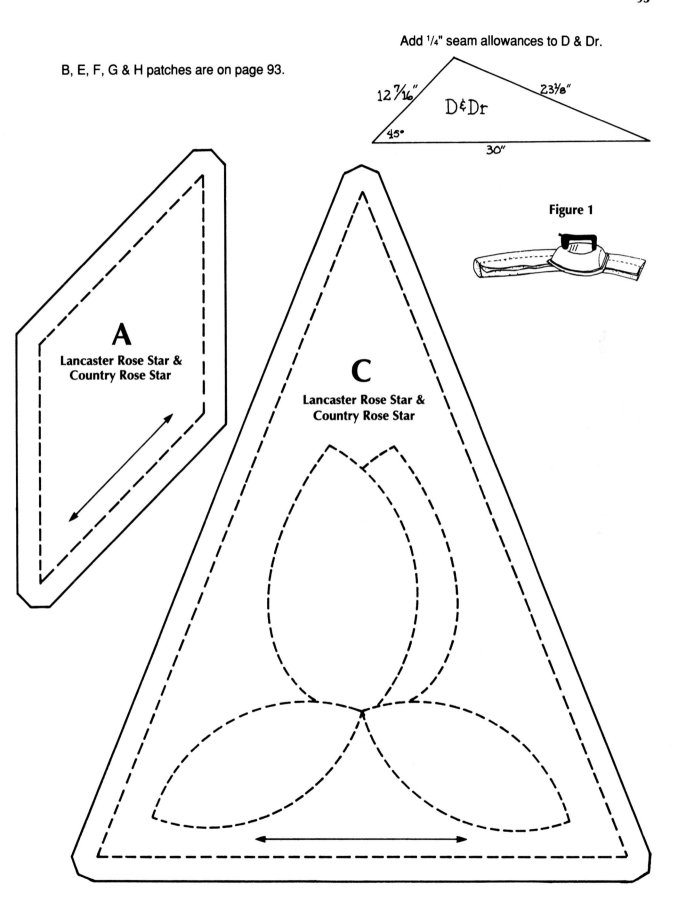

12 ⁷⁄₁₆"   23⅛"

D & Dr

45°

30"

Figure 1

A

**Lancaster Rose Star &
Country Rose Star**

C

**Lancaster Rose Star &
Country Rose Star**

FANCIFUL STAR

Fanciful Star's original look can be credited to two things: the use of fan blocks to fill in the background squares and the use of two diamond sizes, the smaller of which is framed on two sides with darker strips. Colors blend softly from ring to ring, with the occasional ring framed with a darker shade for interest. This quilt is shown in color on page 48. See page 144 for availability of these pastel rainbow fabrics. Color numbers below correspond to color numbers on the fabric bolts.

HINT: Be sure to cut the outermost triangles with the short edge on the straight grain. This will insure that your quilt's edges will be stabilized and will not stretch. Also be sure to backtack the seams here. Otherwise, they could unravel with handling as you quilt.

Yardage (44" fabric) & Cutting Requirements

Diamond Sizes: 2" and 3"
Quilt Size: 55½" x 55½"
¼ yd. Fabric #2: 4 Gr
¼ yd. Fabric #3: 16 B
¼ yd. Fabric #4: 4 G
¼ yd. Fabric #5: 24 C
⅜ yd. Fabric #6: 24 D, 24 E, 4 H
½ yd. Fabric #7: 32 F
¼ yd. Fabric #8: 4 I
¼ yd. Fabric #9: 24 C
⅜ yd. Fabric #10: 24 D, 24 E, 4 Ir
⅜ yd. Fabric #11: 16 F
¼ yd. Fabric #12: 4 Hr
¼ yd. Fabric #13: 8 C
¼ yd. Fabric #14: 8 D, 8 E, 4 Gr
⅜ yd. Fabric #15: 64 B
¼ yd. Fabric #16: 4 G
⅜ yd. Fabric #17: 72 C
1½ yds. Fabric #18: binding 1½" x 6 yds., 72 D, 72 E, 4 H
½ yd. Fabric #19: 80 B
¼ yd. Fabric #20: 4 I
¼ yd. Fabric #22: 4 Ir
¼ yd. Fabric #24: 4 Hr
¾ yd. Fabric #25: 1 A, 8 J, 8 Jr, 16 K
Batting: 59½" x 59½"
Lining: 3⅜ yds.

Referring to block coloring and piecing diagrams, make eight U blocks, four V blocks, four W blocks, four X blocks, four Y blocks, and eight Z blocks (each Z composed of one S and eight T blocks).

Join blocks to form eight wedge-shaped units as shown in the quilt diagram. Sew units to A. Stitch long seams between units.

Complete the quilting pattern for A as follows: Fold a piece of tracing paper in fourths. Trace the motif given in the one-fourth A pattern on page 98 in two opposite quarters. In the other two quarters, turn the paper over to trace the reversed motif. Mark this motif in the A patch. Mark motifs given in G, Gr, H, Hr, I, Ir, J, and Jr patches. Quilt as marked. Quilt "in the ditch" between fan patches except where the quilting motif crosses the seams. Bind to finish.

Quilt Diagram

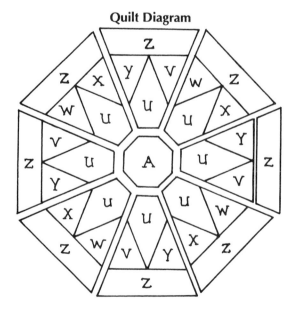

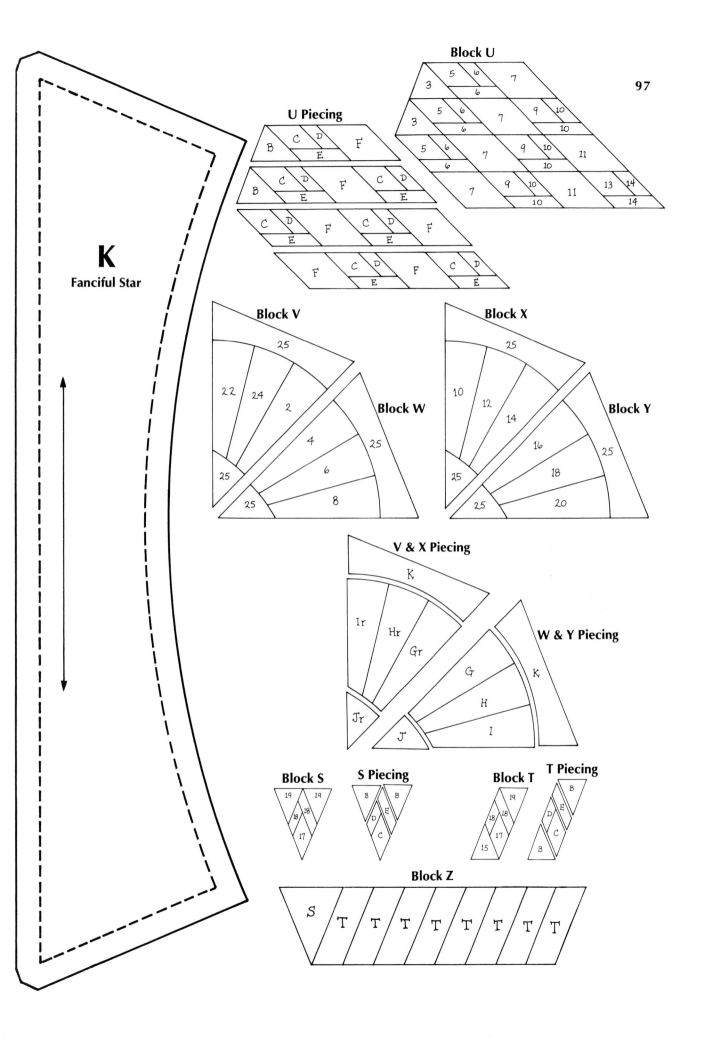

Block U

U Piecing

K

Fanciful Star

Block V

Block X

Block W

Block Y

V & X Piecing

W & Y Piecing

Block S   **S Piecing**   **Block T**   **T Piecing**

Block Z

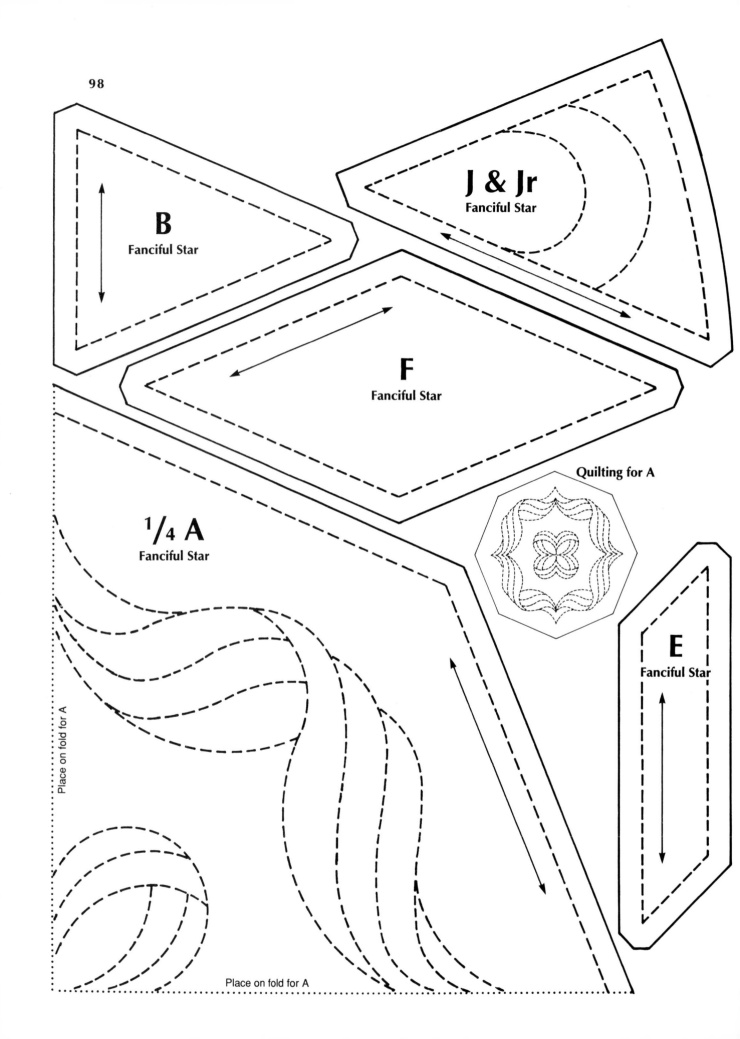

B
Fanciful Star

J & Jr
Fanciful Star

F
Fanciful Star

Quilting for A

1/4 A
Fanciful Star

Place on fold for A

E
Fanciful Star

Place on fold for A

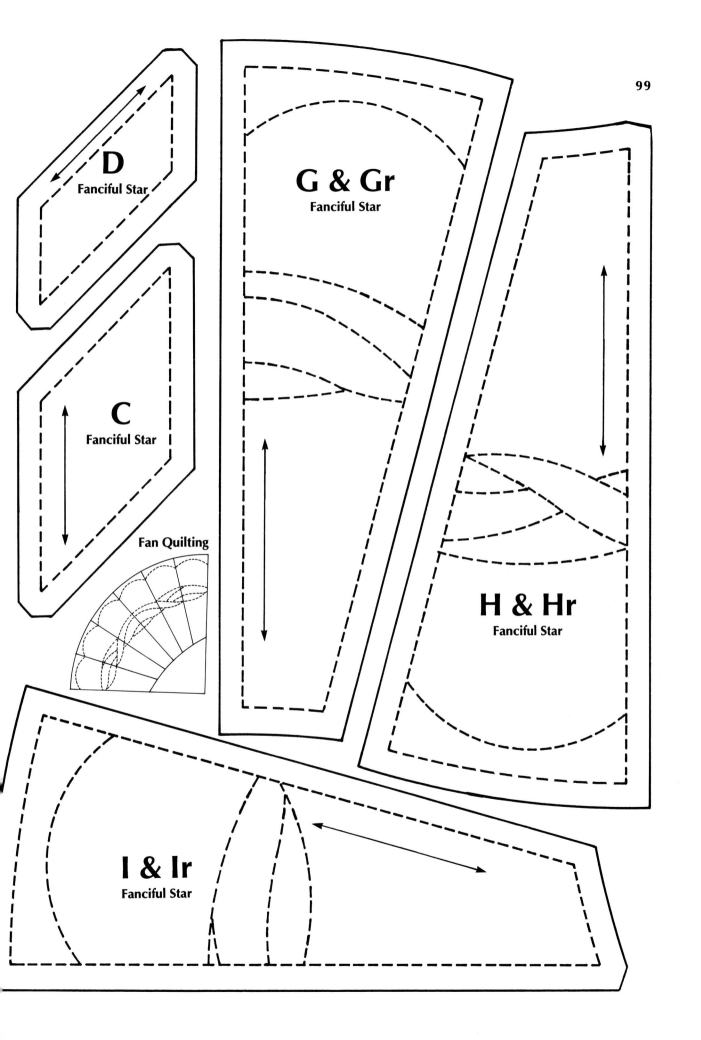

99

D
Fanciful Star

C
Fanciful Star

G & Gr
Fanciful Star

Fan Quilting

H & Hr
Fanciful Star

I & Ir
Fanciful Star

FLYING STAR

A cross between a Lone Star and a Liberty Star, Flying Star is among the fastest made of all the Lone Star variations. A rainbow of pastel colors, each blending into the next, adds color interest to the rich texture of this design. (See the resources list on page 144 for information about availability of rainbow-colored fabrics.) A color photo of the quilt is on page 48.

HINT: This is the easiest of Lone Star quilts to piece if you start by making same-size units. That is, join three A patches to form one large diamond. For the star tips, join four small diamonds (B) to make one large diamond. Once you have made all of these units, simply join them in rows in the usual manner.

Yardage (44" fabric) & Cutting Requirements

Diamond Sizes: $4^{1}/_{2}$" (three $1^{1}/_{2}$" strips) and $2^{1}/_{4}$"
Quilt Size: $52^{1}/_{8}$" x $52^{1}/_{8}$"
$^{3}/_{4}$ **yd. Fabric #1:** binding, $1^{1}/_{2}$" x $6^{1}/_{4}$ yds., 8 A, 16 B
$^{1}/_{4}$ **yd. Fabric #2:** 8 A, 8 B
$^{1}/_{4}$ **yd. Fabric #3:** 8 A
$^{1}/_{4}$ **yd. Fabric #4:** 16 Ar
$^{1}/_{4}$ **yd. Fabric #5:** 16 Ar
$^{1}/_{4}$ **yd. Fabric #6:** 16 Ar
$1^{1}/_{2}$ **yds. Fabric #7:** 4 border strips $1^{1}/_{2}$" x $50^{5}/_{8}$", 24 A
$1^{1}/_{2}$ **yds. Fabric #8:** 4 border strips $1^{1}/_{2}$" x $52^{5}/_{8}$", 24 A
$1^{5}/_{8}$ **yds. Fabric #9:** 4 border strips $1^{1}/_{2}$" x $54^{5}/_{8}$", 24 A
$^{1}/_{4}$ **yd. Fabric #10:** 16 B
$^{3}/_{8}$ **yd. Fabric #11:** 32 B
$^{1}/_{4}$ **yd. Fabric #12:** 24 B
$1^{1}/_{4}$ **yds. Fabric #13:** 4 C, 4 D
Batting: 56" x 56"
Lining: $3^{1}/_{4}$ yds.

Referring to the block diagram, join 3 A's, 3 Ar's, or 4 B's to make $4^{1}/_{2}$" diamonds. Join these diamonds in three rows of three as shown to make a block. Make eight blocks. Join blocks, C's, and D's as shown in quilt diagram.

Join three border strips in order, matching centers. Sew to side of quilt, again matching centers. Repeat for other three sides of quilt. Miter corners, trimming excess from seam allowances.

Complete the quilting motif for C by tracing the motif given in each quarter of a $13^{1}/_{2}$" square. For D quilting, fold a $13^{1}/_{2}$" triangle in half. In one half, trace the flower given on page 101 minus the large leaf. Trace the reverse of this in the other half. Flowers and bases of small leaves should touch center line. Mark quilting in C and D patches. Quilt as marked. Outline quilt the rest of the patches $^{1}/_{4}$" from the seam lines. Quilt $^{1}/_{4}$" from seam lines of border strips. Bind to finish.

Block

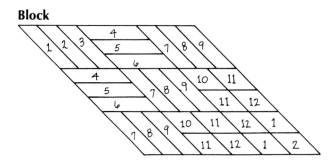

Piecing

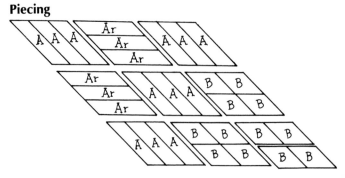

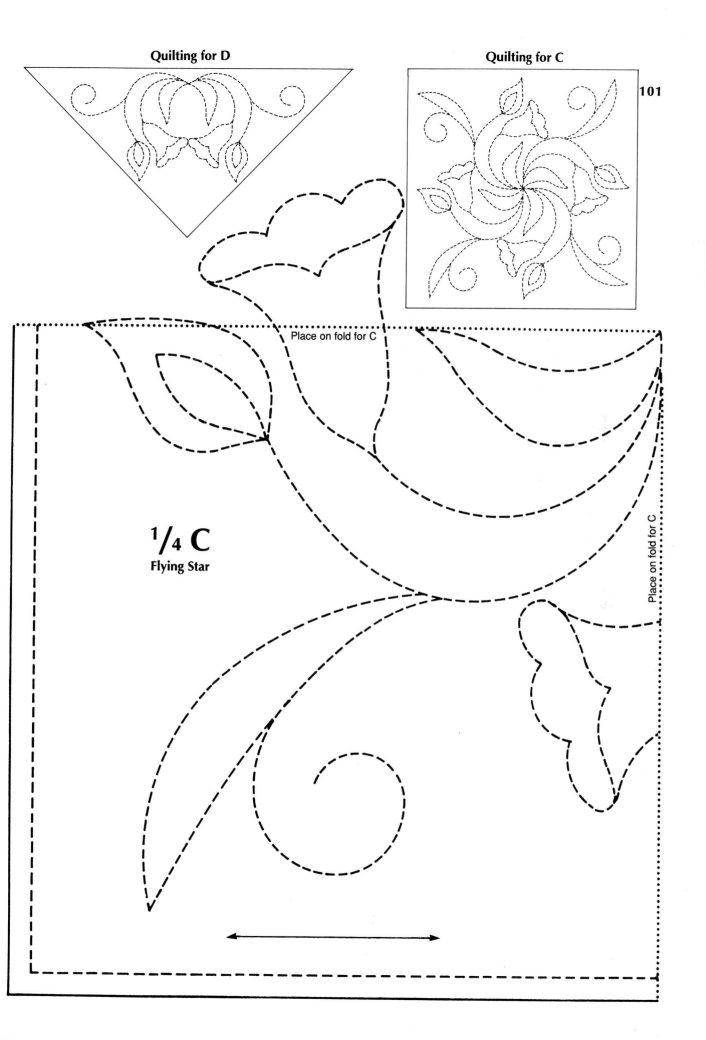

Quilting for D

Quilting for C

Place on fold for C

Place on fold for C

¹/₄ C
Flying Star

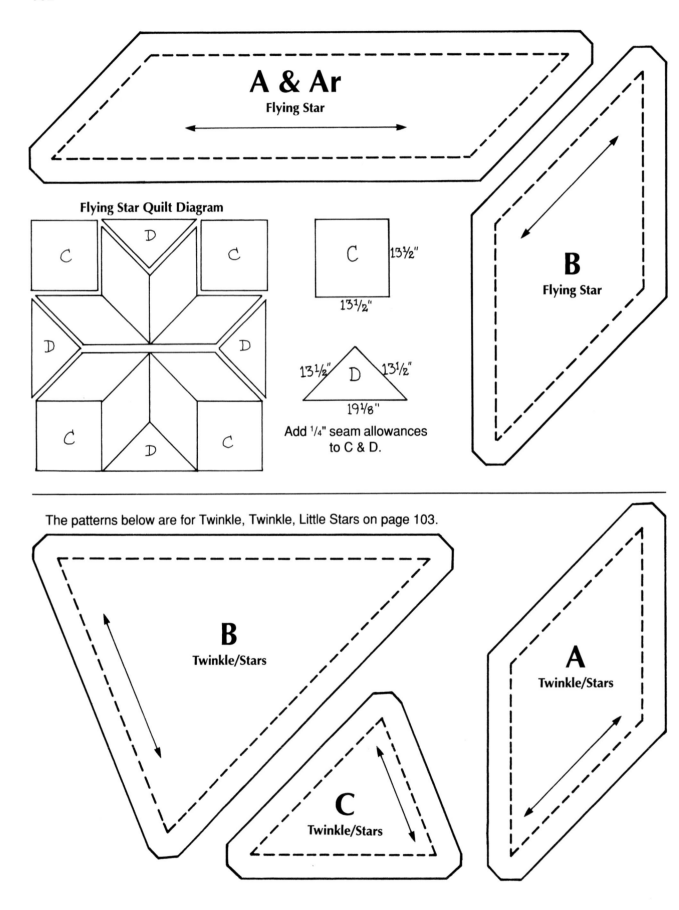

A & Ar

Flying Star

Flying Star Quilt Diagram

C   D   C

D   D

C   D   C

C

13½"

13½"

13½"   D   13½"

19⅛"

Add ¼" seam allowances
to C & D.

B

Flying Star

The patterns below are for Twinkle, Twinkle, Little Stars on page 103.

B
Twinkle/Stars

C
Twinkle/Stars

A
Twinkle/Stars

TWINKLE, TWINKLE, LITTLE STARS

This quilt makes a fascinating sampler of color ideas for Lone Star variations. Even if you don't plan to make this quilt, study the photo on page 56 as you follow the description here to see how different arrangements of color can change the look of the star. Top row: Left, pink and blue star points alternate. Center, the outer two diamonds of the widest ring are colored to match the background for a notched effect. Right, the arrangement of pink and green elements creates an unusual layered effect. Second row: Left, strong contrast emphasizes the center star. Center, the next-to-last ring matches the background and obscures the star. Right, concentric stars, rather than rings, are used here. Third row: Left, busy prints and blending colors make this look more like a Sunburst than a star. Center, the second ring matches the background fabric to make a "space." Right, a hint of a snowflake appears in the center of a strong star, thanks to the use of two different shades of blue. Fourth row: Left, a classic, monochromatic star is framed with a contrasting border. Center, this two-color star uses a large print for transition. Right, alternate-colored diamonds in the center ring form a LeMoyne Star.

HINT: If you plan to try out different color effects in your quilt, be sure to limit your palette to a few colors. This will keep your quilt blocks from looking unrelated and make a more cohesive quilt design.

Yardage (44" fabric) & Cutting Requirements

Diamond Size: 2"
Block Size: 24"
Quilt Size: 78" x 102"
2⅝ yds. Fabric #1: binding 1½" x 10½ yds., 48 D
1⅞ yds. Fabric #2: 48 Dr
3 yds. Fabric #3: 2 border strips 3½" x 104½", 2 border strips 3½" x 80½"
Assorted Scraps: 72 A, 16 B, and 80 C for each block in colors as desired.
Batting: 82" x 106"
Lining: 6⅛ yds.

Referring to diagram, make 12 blocks. Arrange the blocks in four rows of three blocks. Join blocks into rows. Join rows. Add borders, mitering corners and trimming excess from seam allowances.

Mark the quilting motif given in D and Dr patches. Mark four border quilting motifs in the border alongside each block for a total of 16 motifs in each side border and 12 motifs in each top and bottom border. Mark the corner quilting motif in each border corner. Quilt as marked. Quilt "in the ditch" between patches and along border seam lines. Bind to finish.

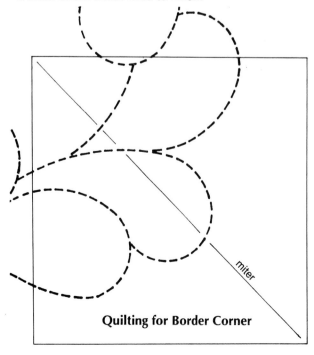

miter

Quilting for Border Corner

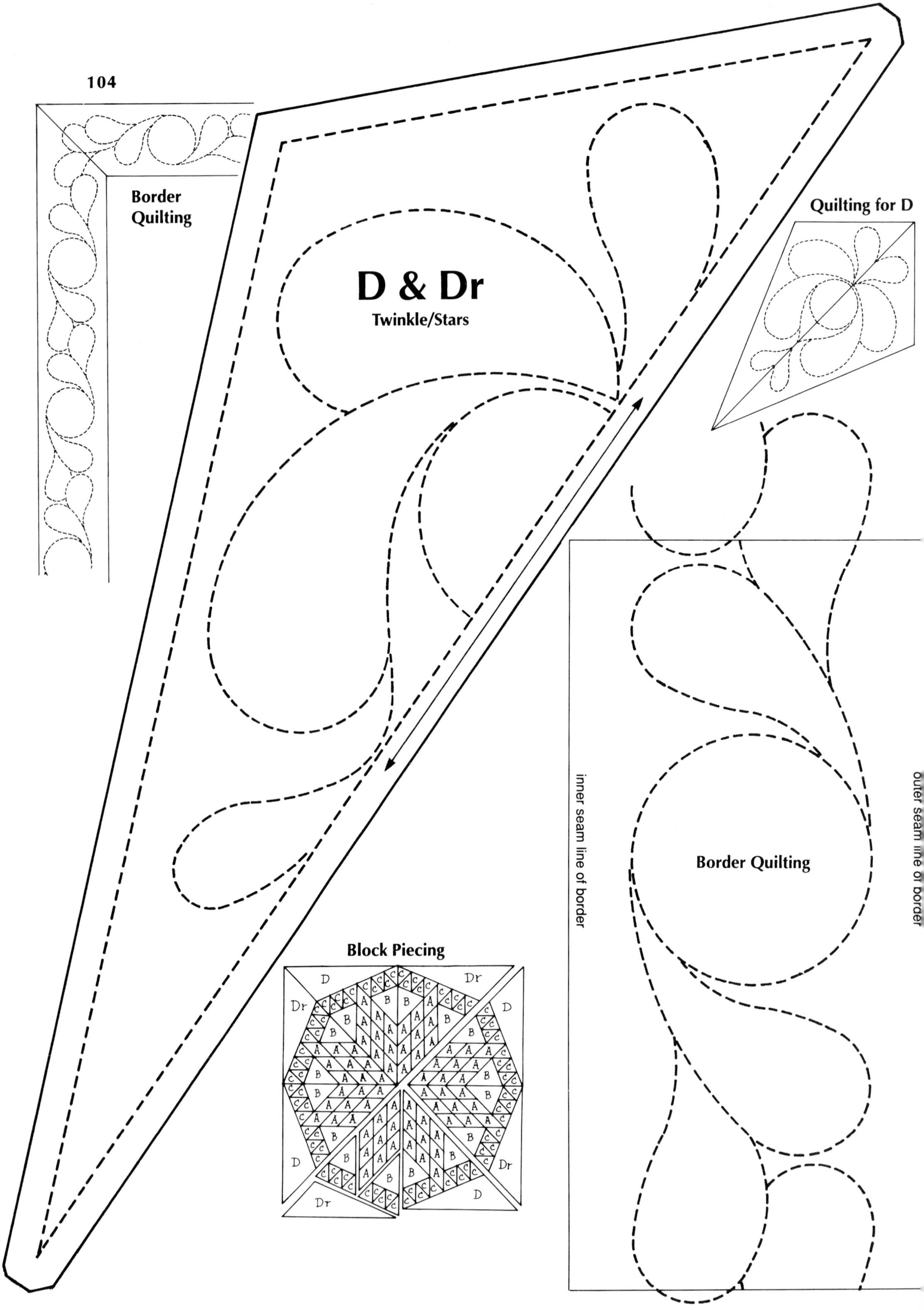
Border
Quilting
D & Dr
Twinkle/Stars
Quilting for D
Border Quilting
inner seam line of border
outer seam line of border
Block Piecing
D
Dr
A
B
C

SUNRISE STAR

Sunrise Star is a handsome arrangement for a Lone Star. The use of progressively darker backgrounds from the central area out plus three different color sequences for the star points help to define three areas: the central star, the pillow and foot extensions, and the borders. See the quilt in color on page 49.

HINT: Fabrics can be cut with care to achieve special effects as in the eight center diamonds of this quilt. Here, each of the eight diamonds is cut from exactly the same part of the print. To test some effects, draw the seam lines of a diamond on tracing paper. Position the diamond over the fabric. Choose an interesting part of the printed motif. Cut out a few diamonds without seam allowances to test the effect. If you prefer, you can conserve fabric by tracing the basic outline of the print onto your paper diamond. Photocopy this several times or trace several copies. Arrange the copies in position next to each other to test the effect. Of course, when you cut the actual fabric diamonds, you will remember to add seam allowances.

Yardage (44" fabric) & Cutting Requirements

Diamond Size: $2^3/_8$"
Quilt Size: $84^1/_4$" x $103^1/_4$"
3 yds. Fabric #1: 2 border strips $3^1/_2$" x $105^3/_4$", 2 border strips $3^1/_2$" x $86^3/_4$", 8 A
$^1/_4$ yd. Fabric #2: 16 A
$^1/_2$ yd. Fabric #3: 60 A
$^5/_8$ yd. Fabric #4: 92 A
$^5/_8$ yd. Fabric #5: 96 A
$^3/_4$ yd. Fabric #6: 124 A
$^7/_8$ yd. Fabric #7: 164 A
$^3/_4$ yd. Fabric #8: 120 A
$^7/_8$ yd. Fabric #9: 144 A
$^1/_4$ yd. Fabric #10: 24 A
$^3/_8$ yd. Fabric #11: 48 A
$^5/_8$ yd. Fabric #12: 6 B, 2 C
$1^3/_8$ yds. Fabric #13: 4 B, 4 C, 2 D
$3^1/_8$ yds. Fabric #14: binding $1^1/_2$" x 11 yds., 8 B, 20 C, 4 E
Batting: $88^1/_2$" x $107^1/_2$"
Lining: $7^5/_8$ yds.

Referring to block coloring and piecing diagrams on page 106, make eight X blocks, twelve Y blocks, and 36 Z blocks.

Join X and Y blocks plus B, C, and D patches as shown in quilt diagram to complete rectangular quilt center.

Join Z blocks plus B, C, and E patches to form four borders as shown. Attach these pieced border strips. Add plain border strips, mitering corners and trimming excess from seam allowances.

Complete the quilting motif for the B square as follows: Fold a $9^1/_2$" square of tracing paper in half diagonally. On one side of the fold, trace the half motif given. Turn the paper over and trace the reversed motif to complete the pattern. See the quarter-quilt diagram on page 106. Mark the completed B motif in the eight corner squares of the inner and outer borders. Also mark this motif in the six B squares above and below the center star and in the two inner corners of each E rectangle. Mark the motif given in the C triangle in all C patches except the eight with long edges toward the quilt center. Quilt as marked. Quilt "in the ditch" around all patches and along border seam lines. Quilt straight lines to connect the tips of diamonds in the remaining squares and triangles and in the D patches. Quilt borders to follow the print or outline quilt $^1/_4$" from seam lines. Bind to finish.

Quilt Diagram

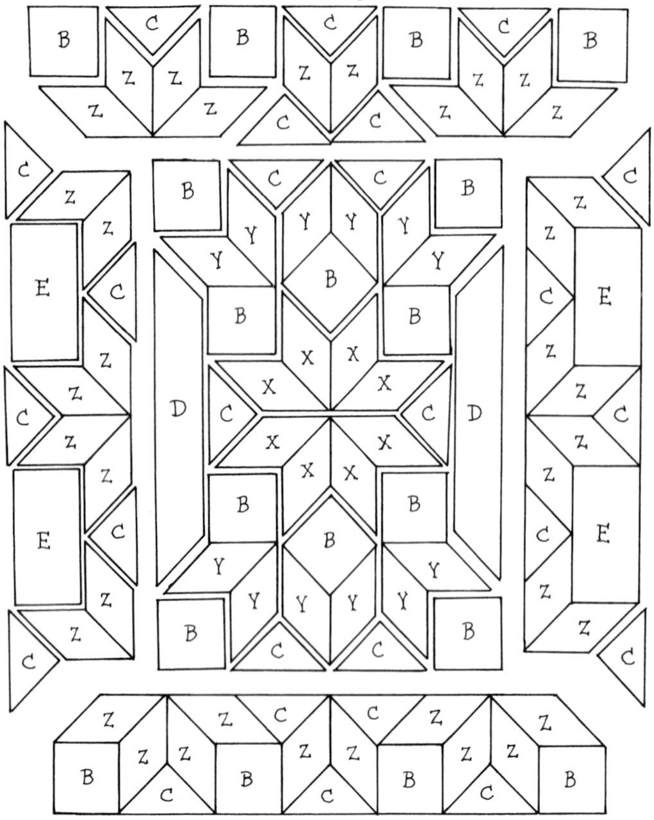

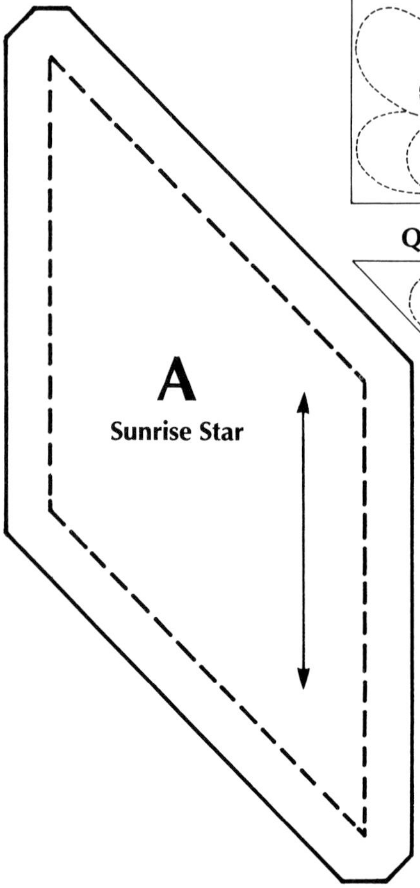

Quilting for B

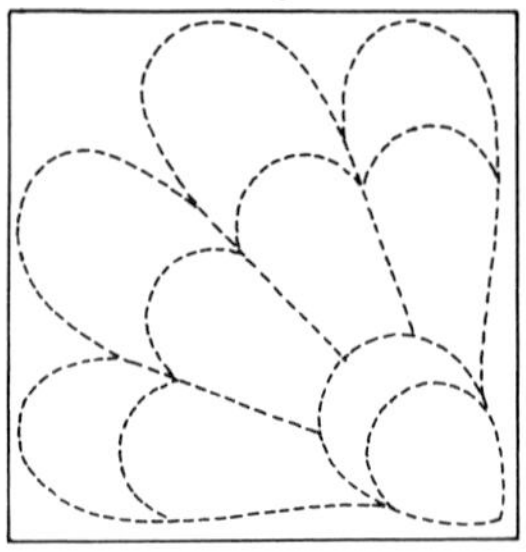

Quilting for C

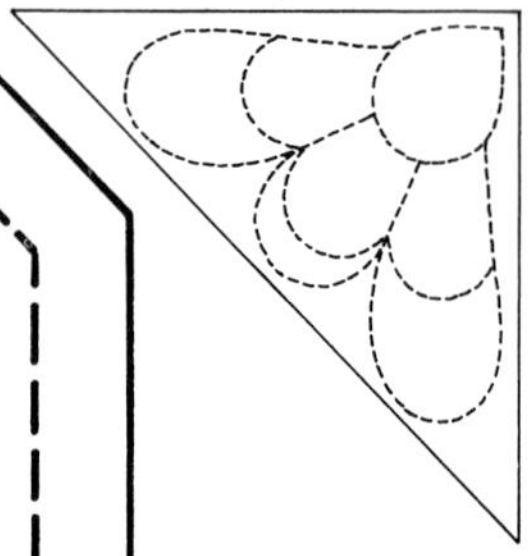

A

Sunrise Star

Add ¼" seam allowances to B, E & D.

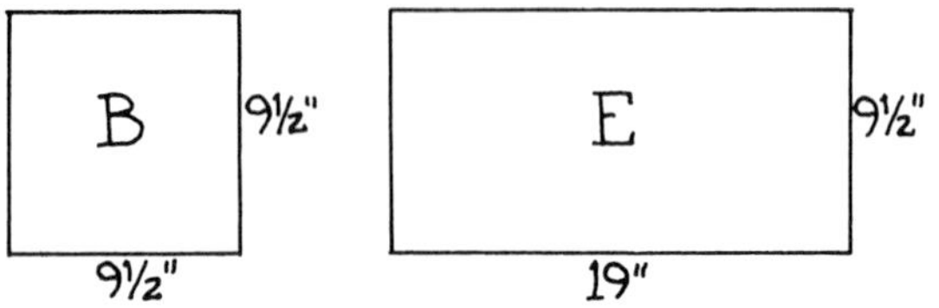

B 9½"
9½"

E 9½"
19"

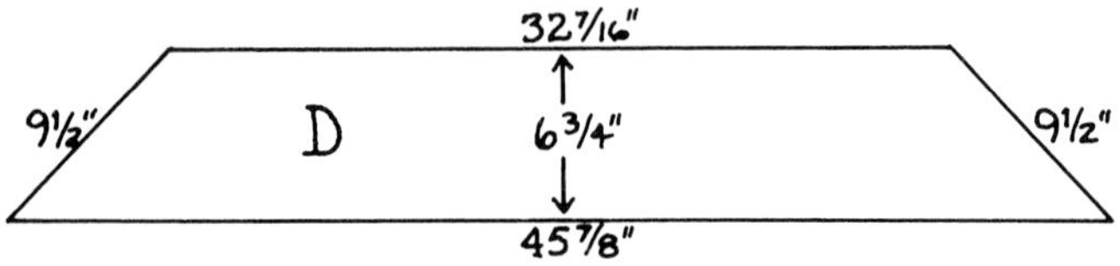

9½" D 9½"
32⁷⁄₁₆"
6¾"
45⁷⁄₈"

Piecing

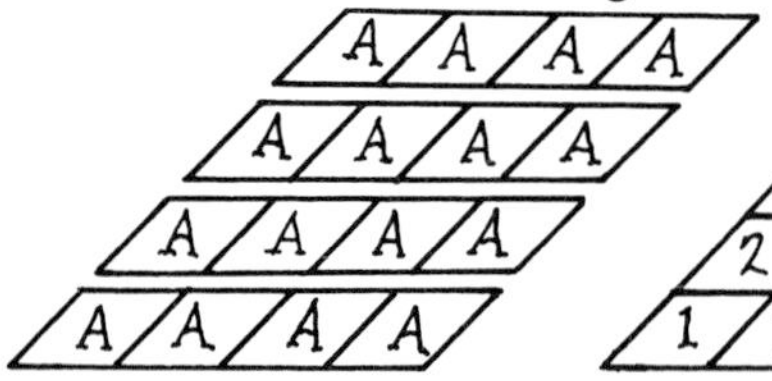

A	A	A	A
A	A	A	A
A	A	A	A
A	A	A	A

Block X

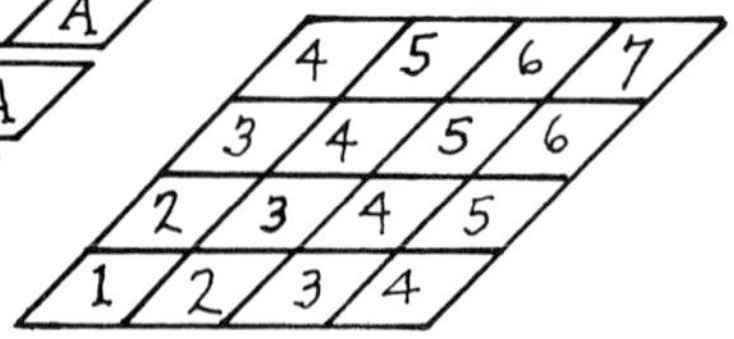

4	5	6	7
3	4	5	6
2	3	4	5
1	2	3	4

Block Y

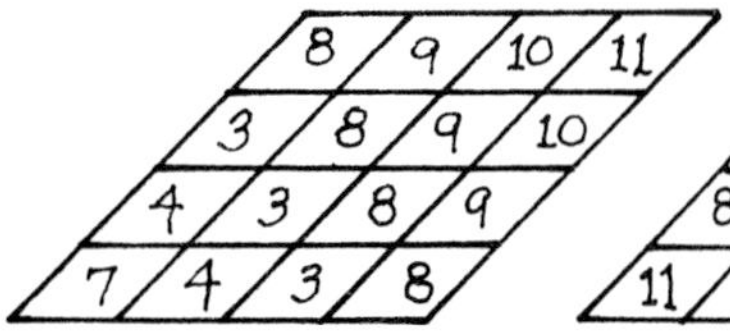

8	9	10	11
3	8	9	10
4	3	8	9
7	4	3	8

Block Z

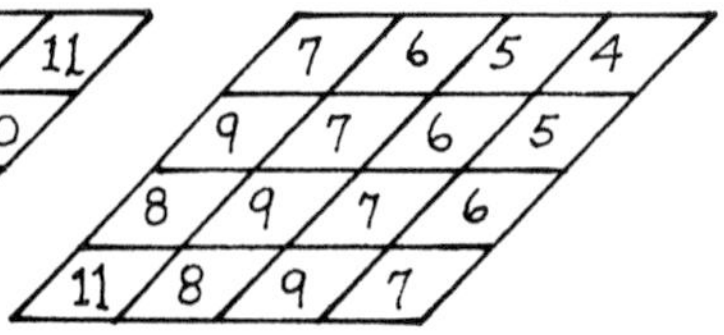

7	6	5	4
9	7	6	5
8	9	7	6
11	8	9	7

Quilting, ¼ of Quilt

Place on fold

Place on fold for C

½ **C**
Sunrise Star

SPRING STAR

Spring Star is a Lone Star embellished with pieced flower blocks. This star looks best made with rings of diamonds that blend at the star tips and with strongly contrasting, plain background fabric. See this quilt in color on page 52.

HINT: To make the flowers stand out from the background, press seam allowances in the flower blocks away from the background. That is, press toward the leaves, stems, and blossoms. Then, when you quilt "in the ditch" in the background alongside the flowers, the flowers will puff out nicely.

Yardage: (44" fabric) & Cutting Requirements

Diamond Size: $2^3/4$"
Flower Block Size: 11"
Quilt Size: $53^1/8$" x $53^1/8$"
$5/8$ yd. Fabric #1: 8 A, 8 I, 8 J, 8 Jr
2 yds. Fabric #2: 16 A, 8 C, 8 Cr, 16 F, 16 G, 8 H, 8 Hr, 8 K, 8 Kr
$3/8$ yd. Fabric #3: 24 A, 8 D, 8 E
$1^1/2$ yds. Fabric #4: 32 A, 8 L
$3/8$ yd. Fabric #5: 24 A, 8 D, 8 E
1 yd. Fabric #6: binding $1^1/2$" x $6^1/2$ yds., 16 A, 8 B
$1/4$ yd. Fabric #7: 8 A
$7/8$ yd. Fabric #8: 8 M
Batting: 57" x 57"
Lining: $3^1/4$ yds.

Referring to diagrams, make 8 Y and 8 Z blocks.
Join blocks plus L's and M's as shown in the quilt diagram.
Complete the quilting pattern for L as follows: Fold a sheet of tracing paper in half. Trace the motif given on one side of the fold. Trace the motif reversed on the other side of the fold. Mark this complete quilting pattern in the L patches. Quilt as marked and outline quilt $1/4$" from seam lines of diamonds and M patches. Quilt "in the ditch" around patches in flower blocks and between L and M patches. Quilt a grid of $3/4$" to 1" squares in the background of the flower blocks, if desired. Bind to finish.

Block Z **Z Piecing**

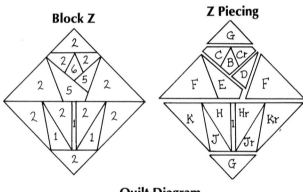

Quilt Diagram

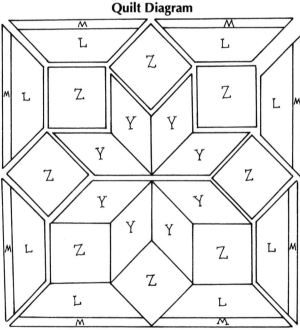

Block Y **Y Piecing**

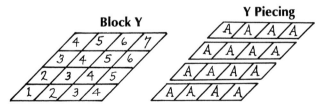

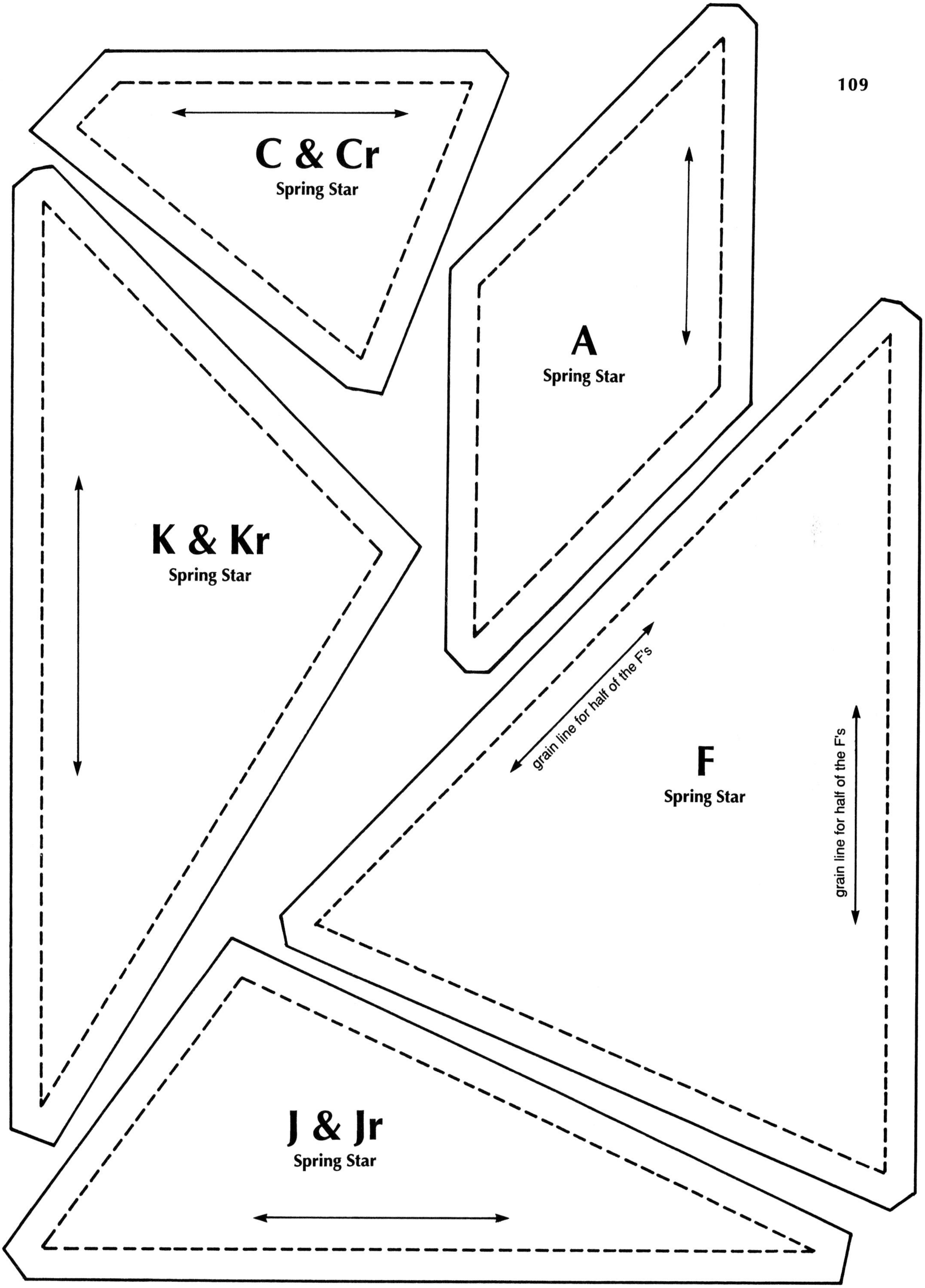

C & Cr
Spring Star

A
Spring Star

K & Kr
Spring Star

grain line for half of the F's

F
Spring Star

grain line for half of the F's

J & Jr
Spring Star

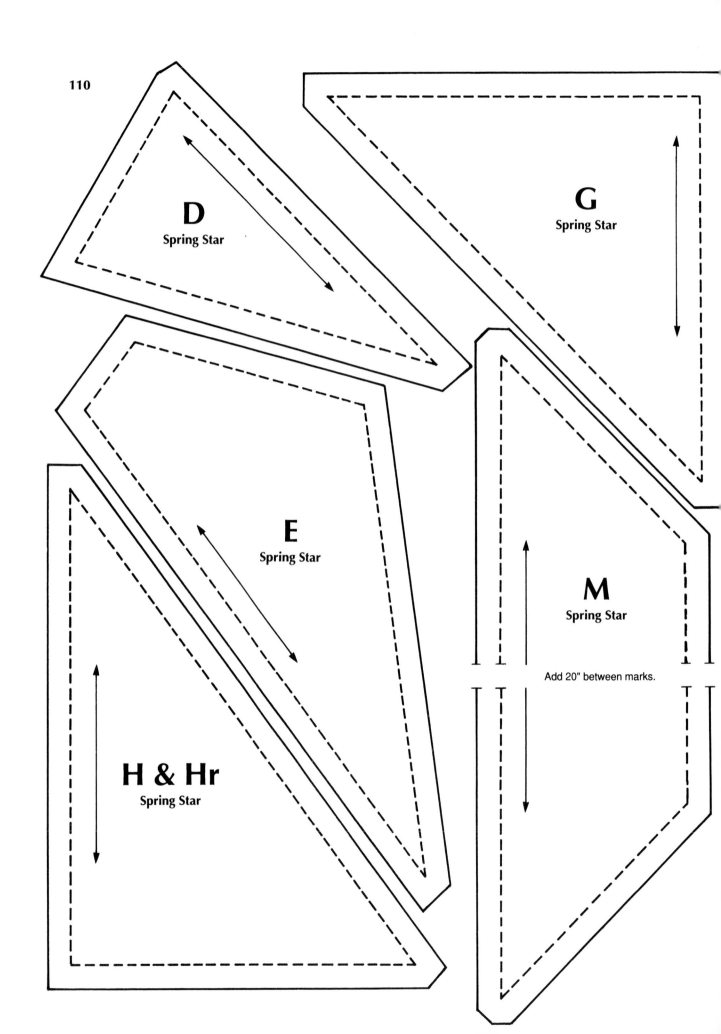

110

D
Spring Star

G
Spring Star

E
Spring Star

M
Spring Star

Add 20" between marks.

H & Hr
Spring Star

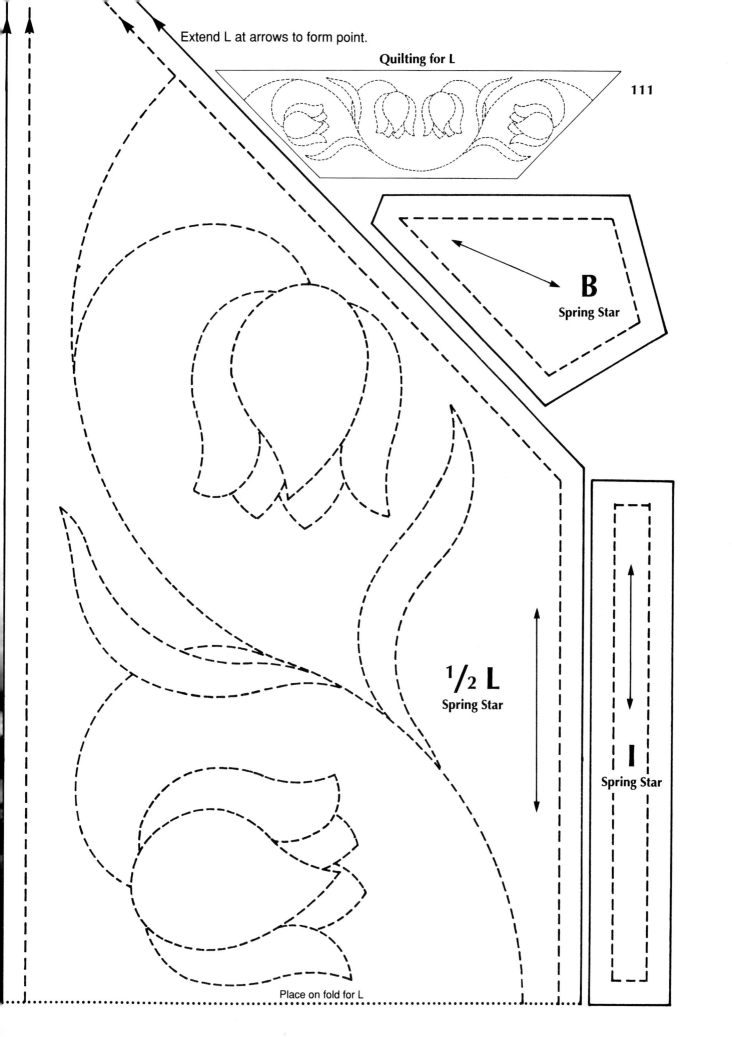

Extend L at arrows to form point.

Quilting for L

111

B
Spring Star

½ L
Spring Star

I
Spring Star

Place on fold for L

EARTH & STARS

Earth & Stars is an appealing Lone Star variation incorporating the star-within-a-star idea. The diamonds for inner and outer stars are similar in color, but varying their sequence gives the inner and outer stars two different looks. For a wall quilt, this design could be made without the pieced borders. A color photo is on page 51.

HINT: The diamond (A) for the center star is six-hundredths of an inch smaller than the diamond (B) for the outer star. Be especially careful to keep the piles of diamonds separate to insure a perfect fit.

Yardage (44" fabric) & Cutting Requirements

Diamond Size: 2.44" and 2¹/₂"
Quilt Size: 95⁵/₈" x 95⁵/₈"
⁵/₈ yd. Fabric #1: 56 A, 16 B
³/₄ yd. Fabric #2: 112 A
2¹/₈ yds. Fabric #3: binding 1¹/₂" x 11¹/₄ yds., 168 A, 80 B
2 yds. Fabric #4: 4 borders 2⁵/₈" x 67¹/₈", 112 A, 64 B
3 yds. Fabric #5: 4 borders 3¹/₂" x 98¹/₈", 56 A, 48 B
¹/₄ yd. Fabric #6: 16 B
2³/₄ yds. Fabric #7: 64 B, 4 C, 4 D, 8 E, 4 F
¹/₂ yd. Fabric #8: 64 B
³/₈ yd. Fabric #9: 48 B
1³/₄ yds. Fabric #10: 8 C, 16 G
Lining: 8¹/₂ yds.
Batting: 99¹/₂" x 99¹/₂"

Note that A diamonds and B diamonds are not quite the same size. Be careful to keep them separate. Referring to diagrams, make 56 Y blocks and 16 Z blocks.

Join eight of the Y blocks

with C's and D's; add Z blocks, E's, and F's to make quilt center as shown in the diagram on page 113.

Make pieced borders as follows: Join remaining Y blocks in sets of four to make 12 half stars. Join half stars with C's and G's to make four border units. Sew plain border strips to inner and outer edges of pieced border units, matching centers. Sew to sides of quilt, again matching centers. Miter corners and trim excess from seam allowances.

Referring to the figure on page 114, complete the quilting motif for G by tracing the D motif from that page in one half and the D motif reversed in the other half of G. Use the motif given on page 115 for both E and F patches. For F, also mark the motif for C (page 113) in the outer corner. Add the middle leaf from D (page 114) to

the left end and the reverse of this leaf to the right end to extend the motif to within 3" of the edges of square F.

Quilt as marked. Use masking tape to mark and quilt a grid of 1" squares in the backgrounds of E and F patches; also add background quilting to C, D, and G patches if desired. Outline quilt the diamonds ¹/₄" from seam lines. Quilt ¹/₄" from long seam lines of borders. Bind to finish.

Block Z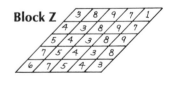

Z Piecing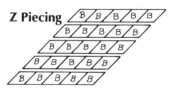

Quilt Center

Block Y

3	4	5
2	3	4
1	2	3

Y Piecing

A	A	A
A	A	A
A	A	A

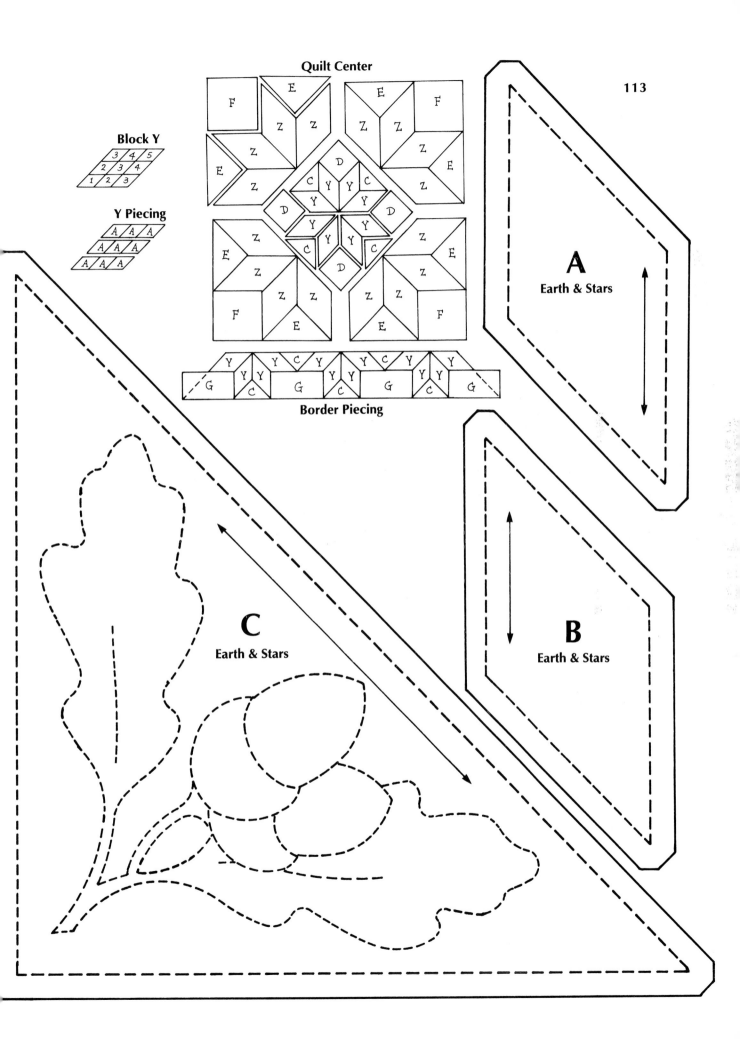

Border Piecing

A
Earth & Stars

B
Earth & Stars

C
Earth & Stars

Quilting for G

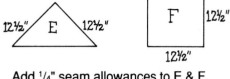

12½"   E   12½"

F   12½"

12½"

Add ¼" seam allowances to E & F.

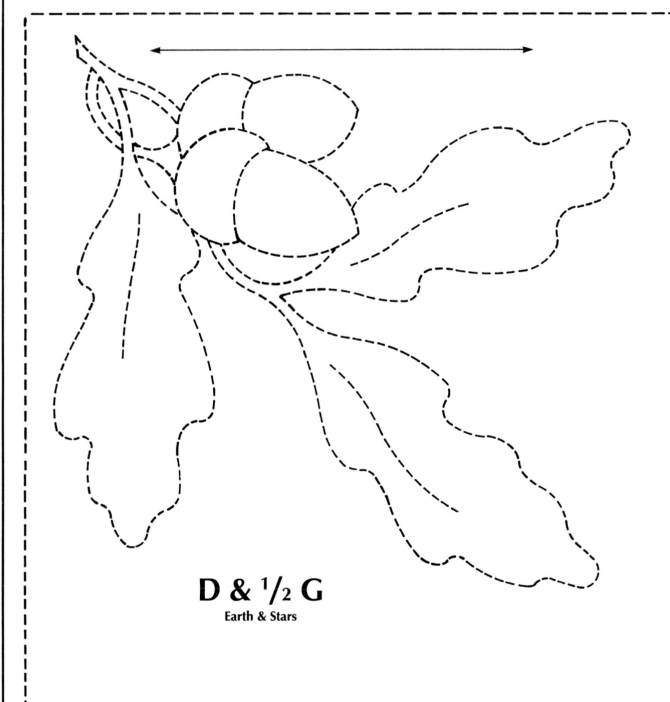

D & ½ G
Earth & Stars

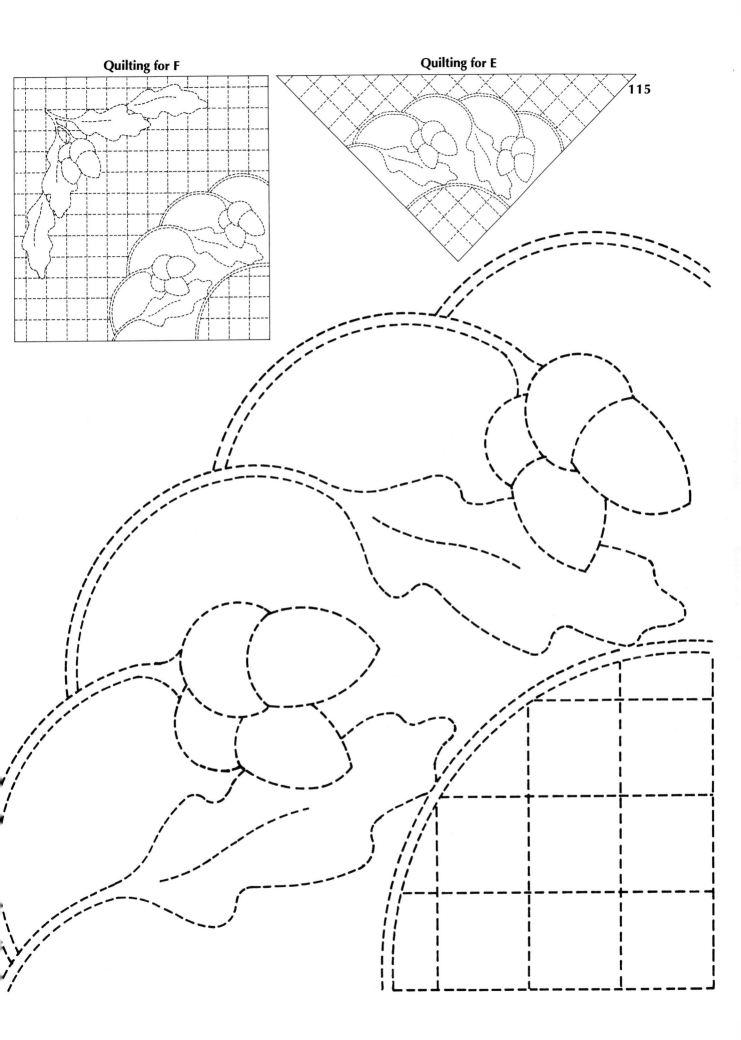

STARBURST

The Sunburst is a traditional Lone Star variation with diamond rings that get larger to the very borders of the quilt rather than tapering into star points. This new sunburst has star points as well for a fresh look. Large and small diamonds, half-diamond triangles, and parallelograms add up to an exciting design that makes a handsome wall quilt or center for a double/queen bed quilt. See this quilt in color on page 50.

HINT: Notice the piecing sequence for the block. Because of the small and large diamonds and the parallelograms, it is not possible to employ the usual rows. However, by making the subunits shown in the block diagrams, you will have no trouble making the blocks and you won't have to set any of the patches into angles.

Yardage (44" fabric) & Cutting Requirements

Diamond Sizes: 2" and 4"
Quilt Size: 68" x 68"
⁵/₈ yd. Fabric #1: 8A, 136 D
⁵/₈ yd. Fabric #2: 144 A
⁵/₈ yd. Fabric #3: 128 A
3 yds. Fabric #4: 16A, 40 B, 4E, 4 Er
⁵/₈ yd. Fabric #5: 128 A
⁵/₈ yd. Fabric #6: 144 A
⁵/₈ yd. Fabric #7: 104 A
¹/₄ yd. Fabric #8: 24 A
³/₈ yd. Fabric #9: 64 A
³/₈ yd. Fabric #10: 72 A
1³/₈ yds. Fabric #11: binding 1¹/₂" x 8 yds., 8 C, 8 Cr, 8 B
Batting: 72" x 72"
Lining: 4¹/₈ yds.

Referring to the diagrams on page 117, join patches as shown to make eight wedge-shaped blocks. Join blocks and E's and Er's as shown in the quilt diagram.

Quilt "in the ditch" around all patches. Use masking tape to mark and quilt a grid of 1" squares in the E and Er patches. Bind to finish.

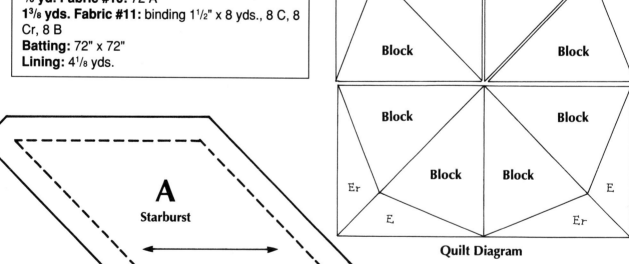

Quilt Diagram

A
Starburst

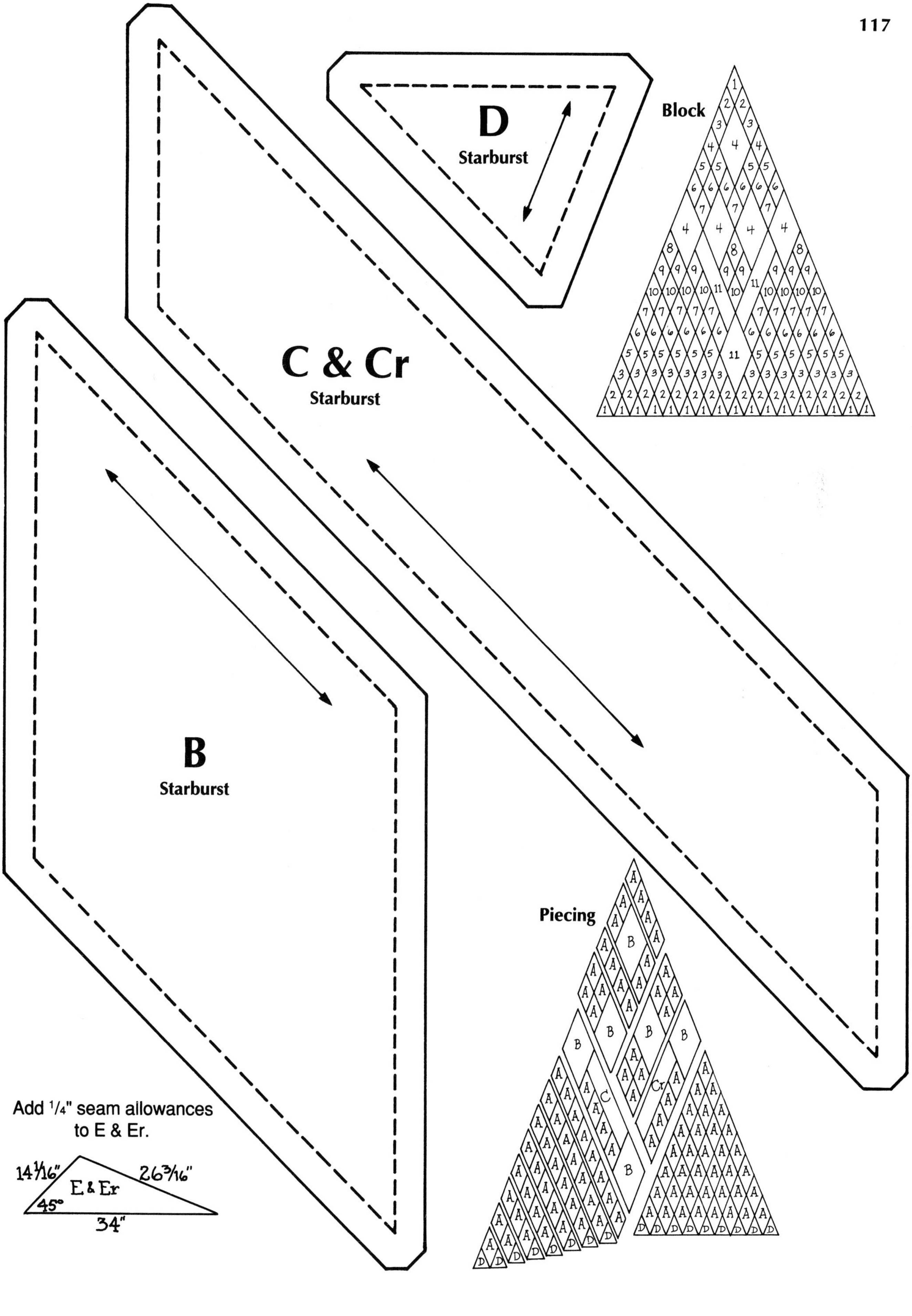

D
Starburst

Block

C & Cr
Starburst

B
Starburst

Piecing

Add ¼" seam allowances
to E & Er.

14¹⁄₁₆"   26³⁄₁₆"
E & Er
45°
34"

MARINER'S STAR

In this Mariner's Star, a Mariner's Compass block replaces the center of the star, and quarter-compass blocks embellish the background squares of a standard Broken Star. Fabrics were chosen carefully in graduated shades to provide both blending and contrast. Find a color photo of this quilt on page 47.

HINT: In a monochromatic (one-color) quilt such as this, avoid the temptation to use only one-color prints. Instead, choose a few prints with accents in other colors. This basically blue quilt has pink accents in some prints. This enlivens the quilt without changing its overall design significantly.

Yardage (44" fabric) and Cutting Requirements

Diamond Size: 2¹/₂"
Quilt Size: 102³/₈" x 102³/₈"
3¹/₄ yds. Fabric #1: binding 1¹/₂" x 12 yds., 224 A, 16 D, 8 G, 8 Gr, 8 I, 8 J, 8 Jr, 8 K, 8 Kr
2¹/₈ yds. Fabric #2: 200 A, 24 D, 8 L, 8 Lr, 8 M, 8 Mr
1³/₄ yds. Fabric #3: 232 A, 48 C
1¹/₄ yds. Fabric #4: 200 A
2¹/₄ yds. Fabric #5: 168 A, 8 H
4¹/₂ yds. Fabric #6: 16 B, 48 E, 8 F, 8 Fr, 8 N, 12 O
Batting: 106¹/₂" x 106¹/₂"
Lining: 9¹/₈ yds.

Referring to block coloring and piecing diagrams, make one W block, eight X blocks, eight Y blocks, and 24 Z blocks.

Sew the X blocks to the W block and stitch the short seams between X blocks. Add Y blocks, Z blocks, plus N and O patches to complete quilt top.

Referring to the figure on page 122, complete the quilting motif for H as follows: Trace the motif given in one half of H, matching dots to add the tip given separately. Trace the motif reversed in the other half of patch.

For N, trace the motif given on page 123 in one half of a 15" triangle; trace the reverse of the motif in the other half to complete the anchor and chain as shown in the figure.

To complete the compass motif, see page 124. One-eighth of a circle is given. Fold a large sheet of paper into eight wedges. Trace the motif given in three alternate wedges. Trace the reverse of the motif in three more wedges. It is not necessary to trace any motif in two wedges, as only three-fourths of a compass is needed. Substitute the long point on page 125 for one point as shown in the figure.

See the figure on page 125. Mark the quilting in the O squares as follows: First, trace the anchor-and-chain motif from N in two of the O's as shown. Next, trace the three-quarter-compass motif across all three O's, stopping at the chain motif. Mark the shell from H in the corner ¹/₂" from the seam lines. Finally, add five wave motifs from page 125 and five reversed waves. Leave off the incomplete waves next to the shell.

Mark quilting motifs in N and H patches. Mark the chain motif given in the 16 E patches of the center pieced compass (W block). Substitute the wave motif on page 121 in the E's of the eight quarter-compasses (Y blocks). Quilt as marked. Quilt "in the ditch" around patches B-K and N. Quilt "in the ditch" around O's except along seam lines joining O's to each other. Outline quilt A, L, Lr, M, and Mr patches ¼" from seam lines. Bind to finish.

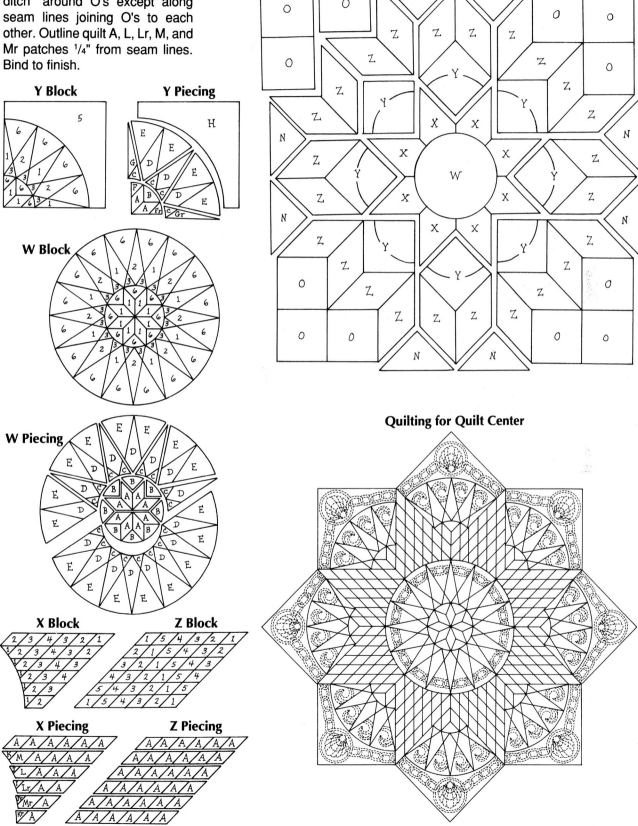

Y Block

Y Piecing

W Block

W Piecing

X Block

Z Block

X Piecing

Z Piecing

Quilt Diagram

Quilting for Quilt Center

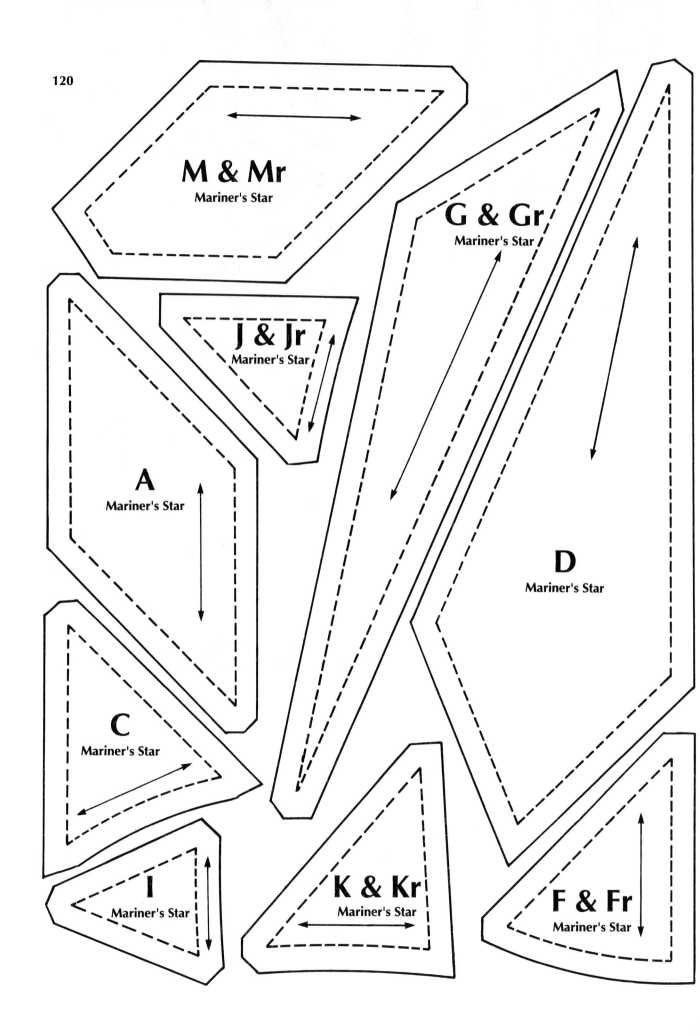

M & Mr
Mariner's Star

G & Gr
Mariner's Star

J & Jr
Mariner's Star

A
Mariner's Star

D
Mariner's Star

C
Mariner's Star

I
Mariner's Star

K & Kr
Mariner's Star

F & Fr
Mariner's Star

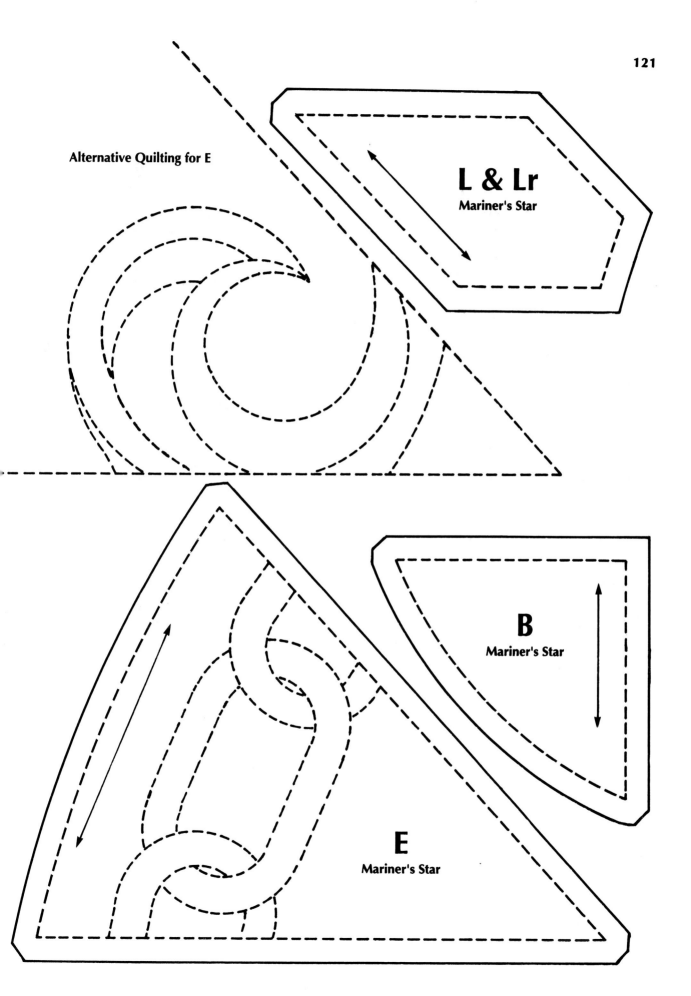

Alternative Quilting for E

L & Lr
Mariner's Star

B
Mariner's Star

E
Mariner's Star

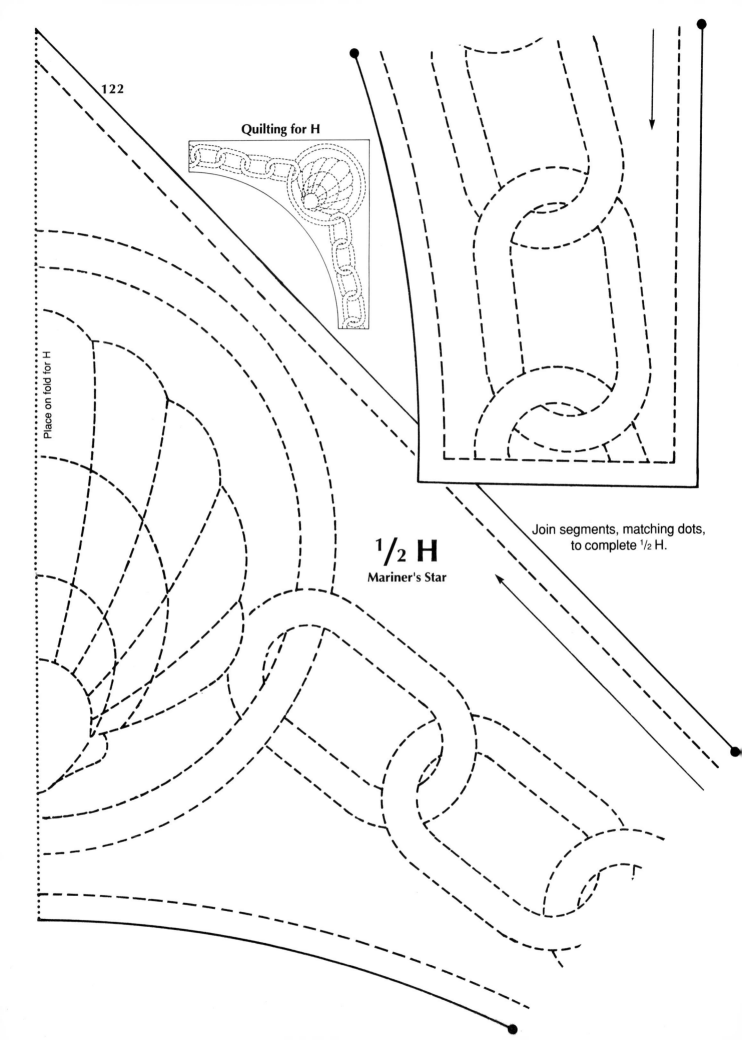

122

Quilting for H

Place on fold for H

½ H

Mariner's Star

Join segments, matching dots,
to complete ½ H.

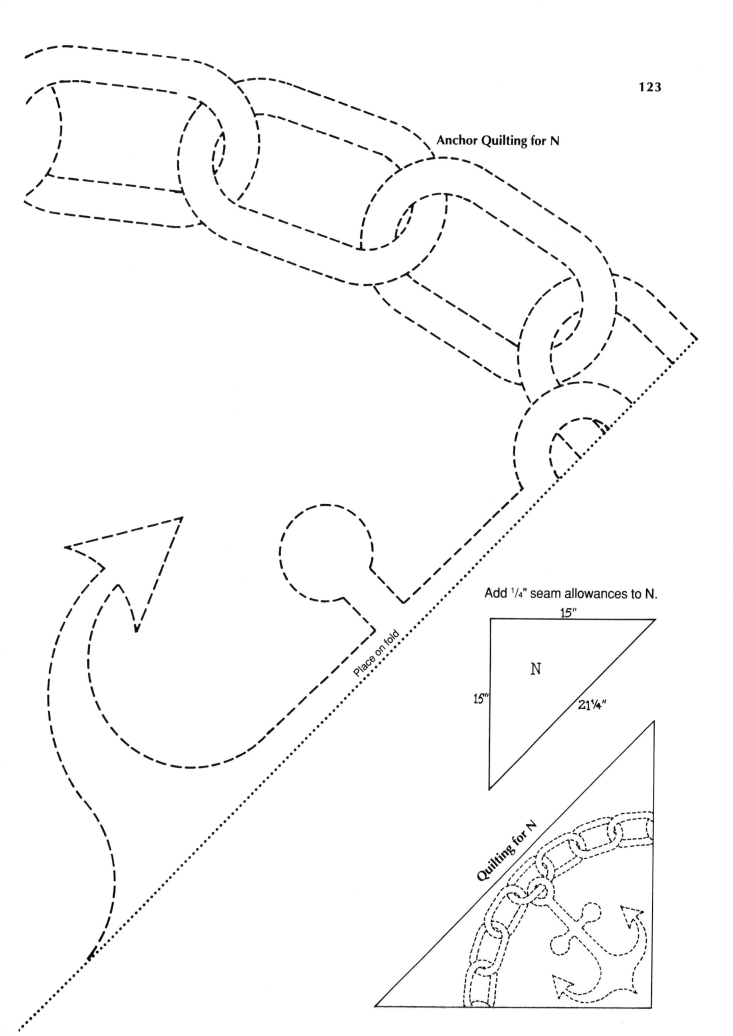

Anchor Quilting for N

Place on fold

Add ¼" seam allowances to N.

15"

N

15"

21¼"

Quilting for N

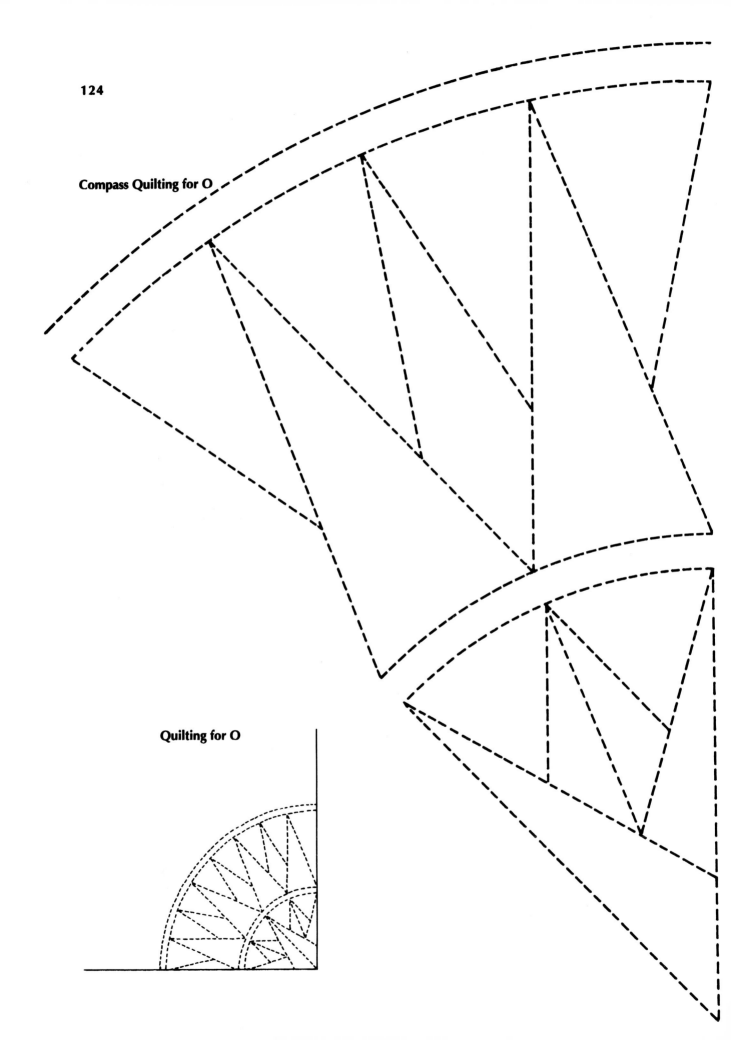

124

Compass Quilting for O

Quilting for O

Corner Quilting of Three O's

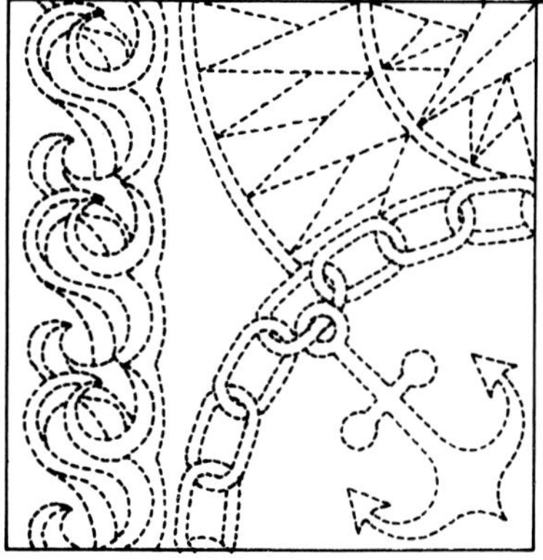

Long Compass Point for O

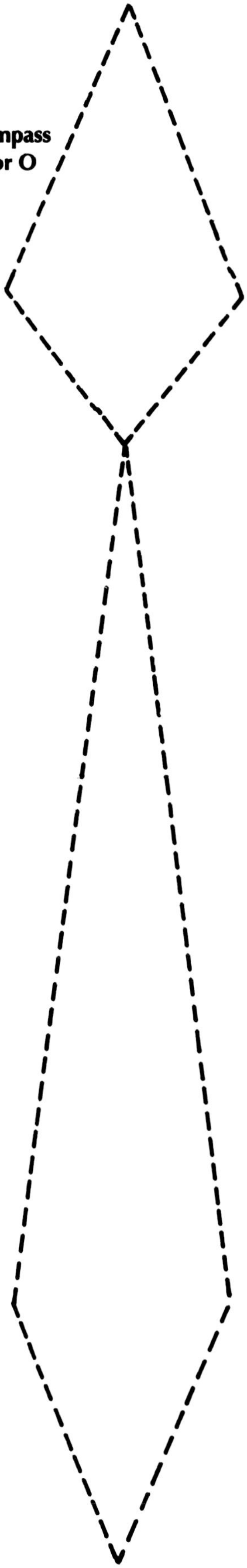

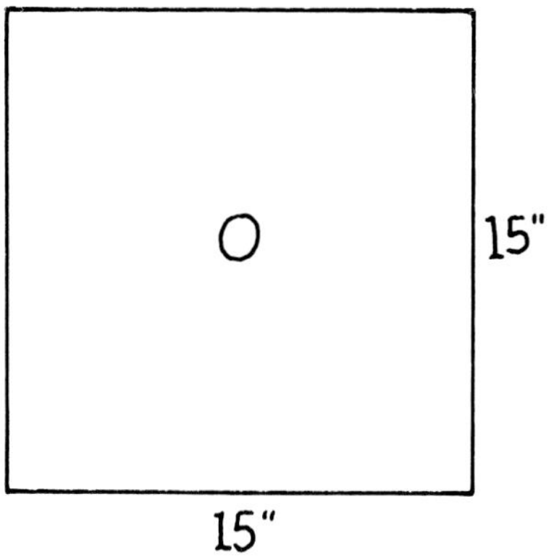

O

15"

15"

Add 1/4" seam allowances to O.

Wave Quilting for O

GEM STAR

Gem Star is a striking wall quilt with the background patches pieced to simulate a border. The star is made of a combination of large and small diamonds plus triangles. Blending and contrasting colors are used to emphasize the octagonal rings. A gracefully curved quilting motif softens the crisp geometry of the design. The color photo of this quilt is on page 52.

HINT: You may prefer to eliminate the seam between large background triangles (D's). This will make the piecing more difficult, but the quilting will be smoother. For this variation, make the star points and join them to complete the star. Sew the "borders" to two sides of each kite-shaped D-D patch. Insert the bordered patches between star points.

Yardage (44" fabric) & Cutting Requirements

Diamond Sizes: 1³/₄" and 3¹/₂"
Quilt Size: 64³/₄" x 64³/₄"
¹/₈ **yd. Fabric #1:** 16 A
¹/₈ **yd. Fabric #2:** 16 A
⁷/₈ **yd. Fabric #3:** 16 C, 16 D
¹/₄ **yd. Fabric #4:** 16 C
³/₈ **yd. Fabric #5:** 48 A
³/₈ **yd. Fabric #6:** 48 A
³/₈ **yd. Fabric #7:** 32 C
³/₈ **yd. Fabric #8:** 32 C
³/₈ **yd. Fabric #9:** 80 A
³/₈ **yd. Fabric #10:** 80 A
¹/₂ **yd. Fabric #11:** 32 B
³/₈ **yd. Fabric #12:** 48 A
³/₈ **yd. Fabric #13:** 48 A
³/₈ **yd. Fabric #14:** 16 B
³/₄ **yd. Fabric #15:** binding 1¹/₂" x 7 yds., 16 A
⁷/₈ **yd. Fabric #16:** 16 A, 64 B
⁷/₈ **yd. Fabric #17:** 128 C
Batting: 69" x 69"
Lining: 4 yds.

Referring to diagrams, join small A diamonds in sets of four to make larger diamonds the size of B. Also join C's in pairs to form large diamonds. Join these, along with B's, in rows as shown. Join rows to complete a Y block. Make eight Y blocks.

For "borders," join B's and C's; add D to complete triangular Z block. Make sixteen of these blocks. Sew two to each Y block to complete eight wedges.

Join four wedges to make half of quilt. Repeat. Join halves.

Mark and quilt the tulip motif on page 128, centering the motif over two adjacent D's as shown in the figure. Outline quilt the B and C patches. Quilt "in the ditch" around A's. Bind to finish.

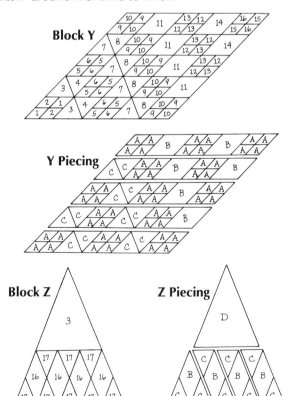

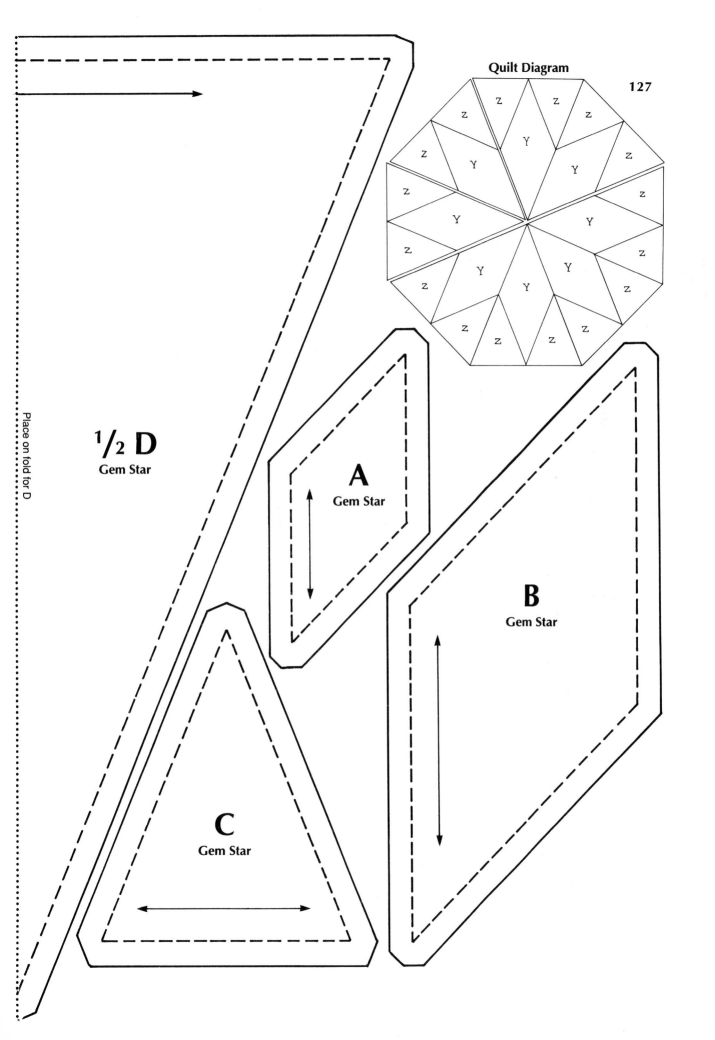

Quilt Diagram

¹/₂ D
Gem Star

Place on fold for D

A
Gem Star

B
Gem Star

C
Gem Star

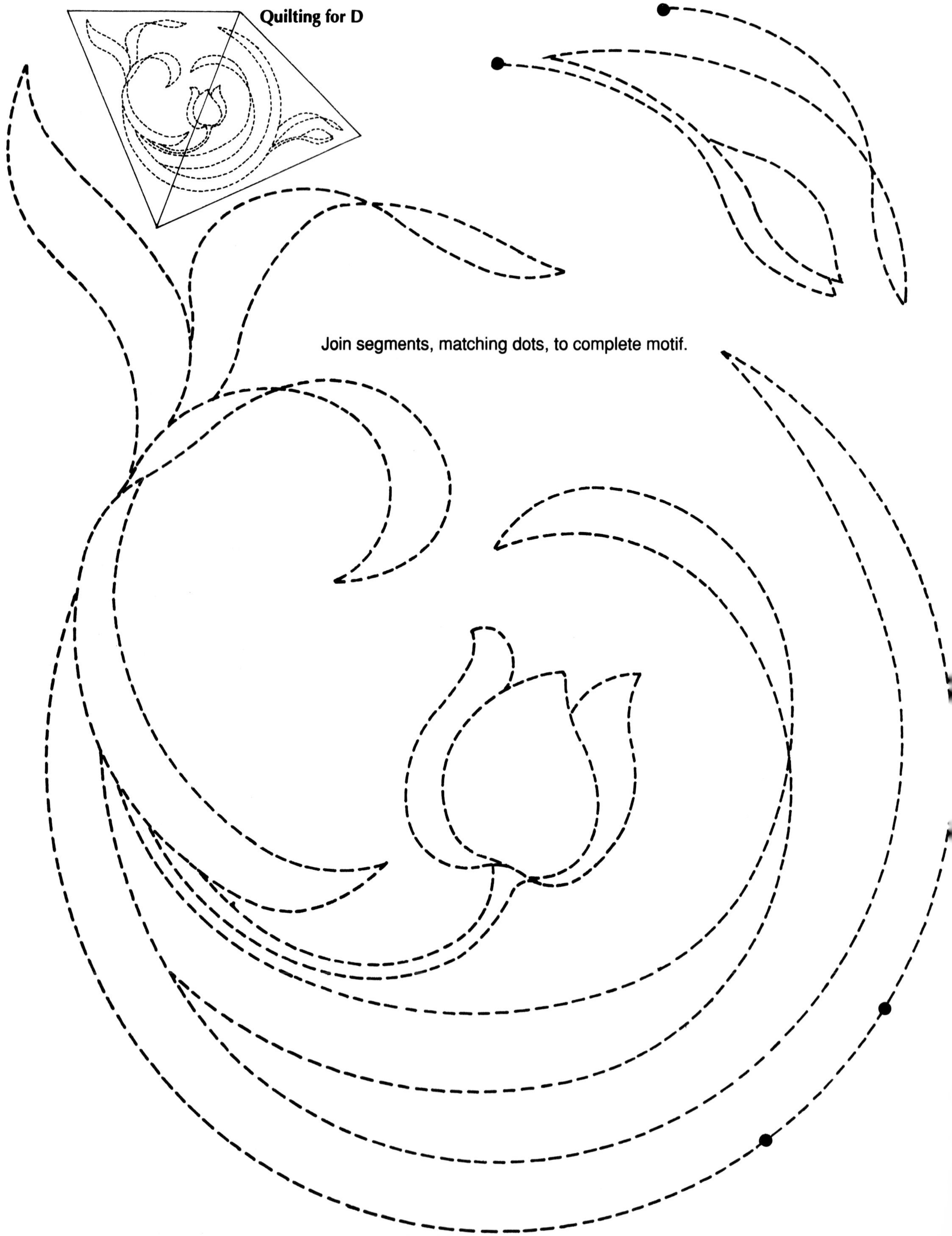

Quilting for D

Join segments, matching dots, to complete motif.

STAR OF LOVE

Star of Love is a Lone Star variation arranged like a Farmer's Daughter block. Star points are separated by appliqued blocks. By choosing a background fabric for the applique blocks to contrast sharply with the background trapezoids (J's), you will get a totally different effect from the low-contrast look here. This quilt is in color on page 46.

HINT: Cut the dark brown heart-shaped appliques around the outside only. Applique the light brown shapes over them; then cut away the dark brown from behind the light brown. After cutting away excess, applique the whole shape to the background block. It is easier to applique the motif for the center block as one four-lobed patch rather than four smaller patches.

Yardage (44" fabric) & Cutting Requirements

Diamond Size: 2"
Quilt Size: 58" x 58"
Block Size: 12"
1/4 yd. Fabric #1: 8 A
1/4 yd. Fabric #2: 16 A
1/4 yd. Fabric #3: 24 A
1³/₄ yds. Fabric #4: 4 border strips 3" x 60¹/₂", 32 A, 24 H
1 yd. Fabric #5: binding 1¹/₂" x 7 yds., 48 A, 12 H
³/₈ yd. Fabric #6: 48 A
¹/₂ yd. Fabric #7: 40 A, 12 G, 4 I
¹/₂ yd. Fabric #8: bias stripping ³/₄" x 3 yds. for stems, 32 A
⁵/₈ yd. Fabric #9: 24 A, 4 D, 1 F
³/₄ yd. Fabric #10: 16 A, 4 C, 1 E
³/₄ yd. Fabric #11: 4 B
1⁵/₈ yds. Fabric #12: 5 B, 4 J
Batting: 62" x 62"
Lining: 3⁵/₈ yds.

Referring to block coloring and piecing diagrams, make eight Z blocks.

Turn under edges of applique patches ³/₁₆" and baste. Make stems by folding bias stripping in half lengthwise with right sides out. Stitch ¹/₈" from raw edges. Press to conceal seam under strip. Cut into four 12" lengths, four 9¹/₄" lengths, and four 3" lengths. Position appliques on B patches and blindstitch in alphabetical order to complete one X block and four Y blocks as shown.

Join blocks, B's, and J's as shown in the quilt diagram.

Mark the heart quilting as follows: In each J patch, mark three hearts, overlapping them and deleting the lines of one heart where the other heart overlaps it (as shown on page 133). In each of the four corner B squares, mark four interlocked heart motifs as shown. Quilt as marked. Quilt "in the ditch" around all patches, including appliques. Bind to finish.

Quilt Diagram

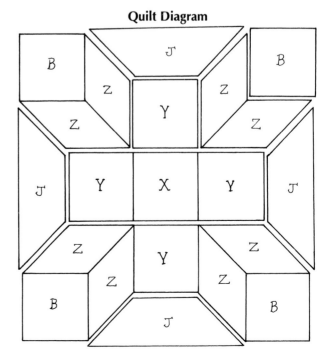

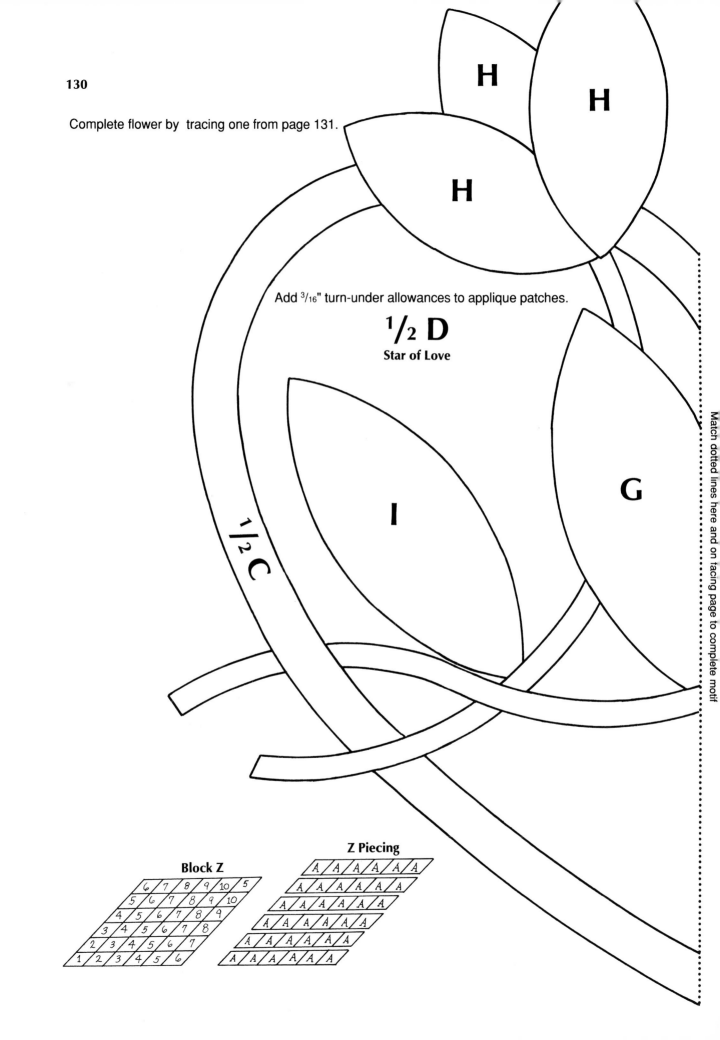

Complete flower by tracing one from page 131.

Add ³/₁₆" turn-under allowances to applique patches.

½ D
Star of Love

½ C

I

G

H

H

H

Match dotted lines here and on facing page to complete motif

Block Z

6	7	8	9	10	5
5	6	7	8	9	10
4	5	6	7	8	9
3	4	5	6	7	8
2	3	4	5	6	7
1	2	3	4	5	6

Z Piecing

A	A	A	A	A	A
A	A	A	A	A	A
A	A	A	A	A	A
A	A	A	A	A	A
A	A	A	A	A	A
A	A	A	A	A	A

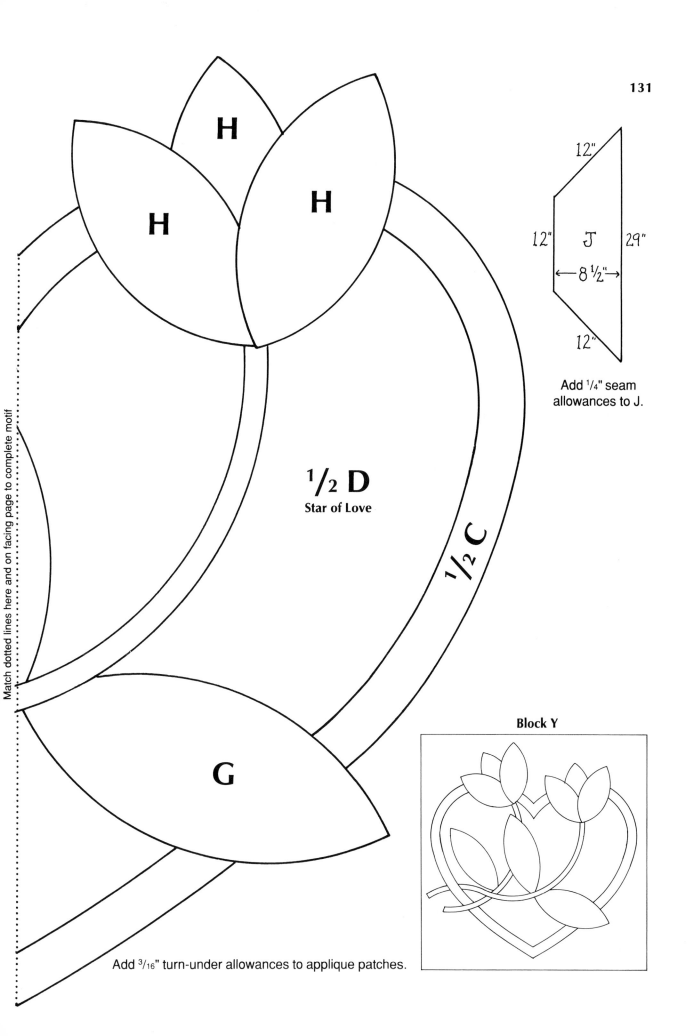

H

H

H

Match dotted lines here and on facing page to complete motif

¹/₂ D
Star of Love

¹/₂ C

G

12"

12" J 29"

← 8 ¹/₂" →

12"

Add ¹/₄" seam
allowances to J.

Block Y

Add ³/₁₆" turn-under allowances to applique patches.

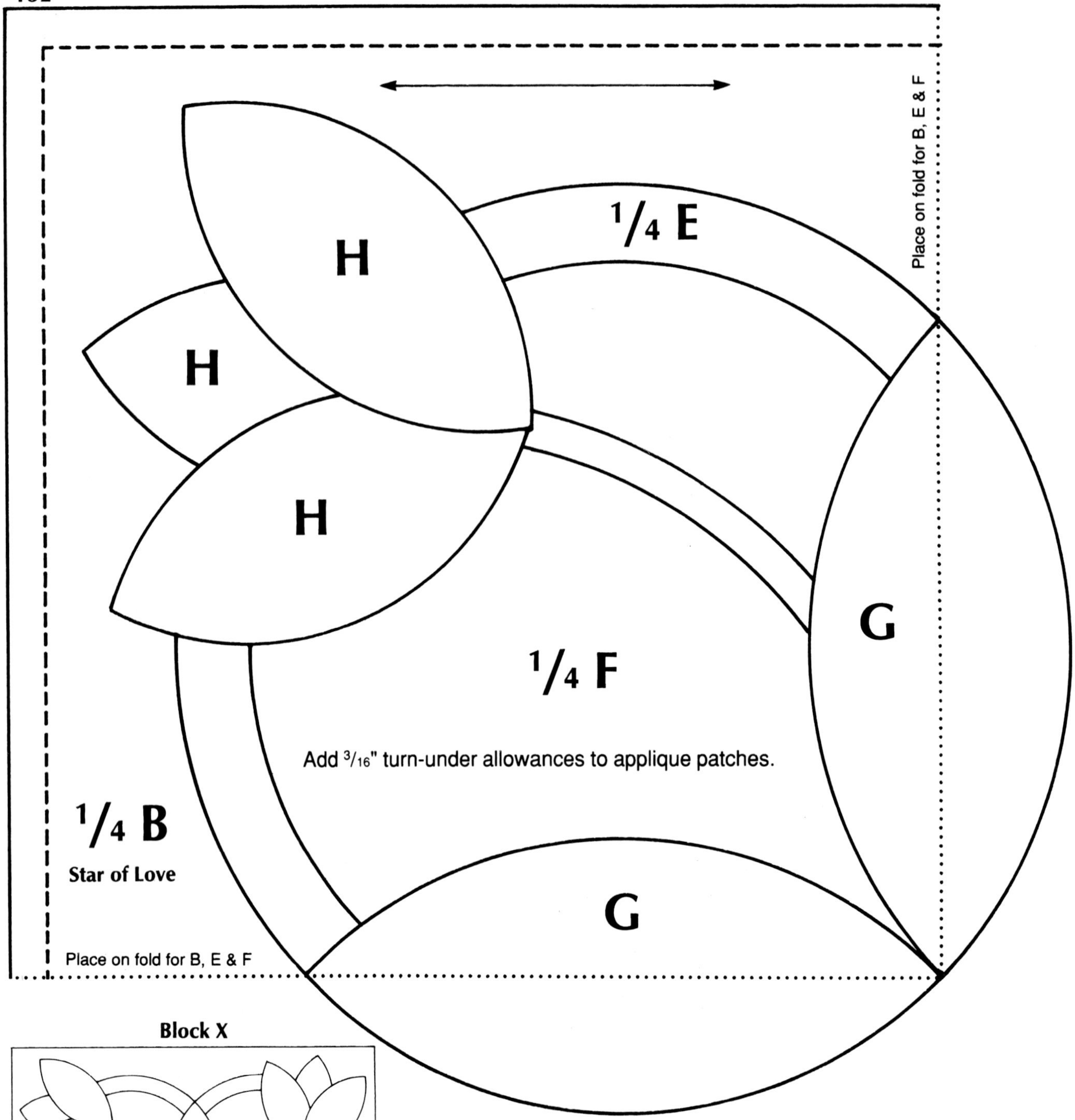

Place on fold for B, E & F

H

H

H

¹/₄ E

G

¹/₄ F

Add ³/₁₆" turn-under allowances to applique patches.

¹/₄ B

Star of Love

Place on fold for B, E & F

G

Block X

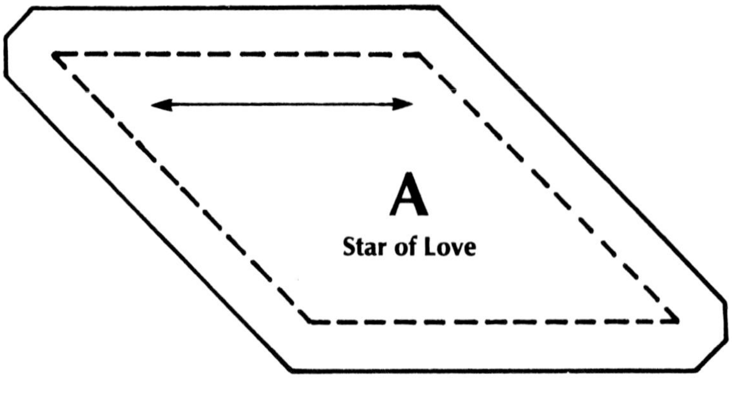

A

Star of Love

Quilting for B

Quilting for J

RADIANT STAR

Radiant Star is a unique, sixteen-pointed Lone Star. Because of the change in color emphasis from red to blue, we see a smaller eight-pointed Lone Star within the larger star. Graduated shades of two very different colors are perfect for this pattern. A handsome pieced border adds the finishing touch. Radiant Star is shown in color on page 53.

HINT: Measure the quilt top and the pieced border carefully and trim the plain border strips to fit before attaching them.

Yardage (44" fabric) & Cutting Requirements

Diamond Size: 2³/₄"
Quilt Size: 98" x 98"
¹/₄ **yd. Fabric #1:** 8 A
¹/₄ **yd. Fabric #2:** 16 A
³/₈ **yd. Fabric #3:** 24 A
³/₈ **yd. Fabric #4:** 32 A
³/₈ **yd. Fabric #5:** 40 A
³/₈ **yd. Fabric #6:** 32 A
³/₈ **yd. Fabric #7:** 24 A
¹/₄ **yd. Fabric #8:** 16 A
¹/₄ **yd. Fabric #9:** 8 A
1¹/₄ **yds. Fabric #10:** 176 A
1³/₈ **yds. Fabric #11:** 192 A
³/₈ **yd. Fabric #12:** 48 A
2³/₄ **yds. Fabric #13:** 64 A, 144 E, 4 F, 4 Fr
4 **yds. Fabric #14:** 80 A, 8 B, 8 C, 4 D
¹/₂ **yd. Fabric #15:** 64 A
2³/₈ **yds. Fabric #16:** 4 border strips 2¹/₄" x 80³/₈", binding 1¹/₂" x 11¹/₂ yds., 48 A
³/₈ **yd. Fabric #17:** 32 A
¹/₄ **yd. Fabric #18:** 16 A
Batting: 102" x 102"
Lining: 8³/₄ yds.

Complete the pattern for C by adding the tip (given separately), matching dots. Referring to block and piecing diagrams, make eight V blocks and 16 W blocks. Join one V block with two W blocks and a C patch to form a unit. Repeat to make eight units (one is shown in gray in quilt diagram).

Join units as shown. Insert eight B's around star to complete octagon. Add four corner triangles (D). Add plain border strips, mitering corners and trimming excess from seam allowances.

Make pieced border as follows: Make 68 X blocks, four Y blocks, and four Z blocks as shown. Join 17 X blocks in a row. Sew a Y to the left end and a Z to the right end. Add F and Fr as shown in the border figure. Sew to side of quilt. Repeat for remaining three sides. Join at corners. Insert F and Fr patches into angles at corners of quilt.

To complete the quilting motif for the B triangle, see the figure on page 136. Trace the large heart and flower from C. Add one tendril (from page 136) and one tendril reversed, matching dots and squares. For the D triangles, see the figure on page 137. Trace the flower from the C motif on the midline of the triangle, 1¹/₂" from the long edge. Also on the midline, trace a flower center and three petals as shown in the figure. The petals should be ¹/₄" from seam lines. Trace eight small hearts from the C motif. Add one tendril and one tendril reversed to complete the motif as shown. Mark the quilting motifs in B, C, and D patches. Quilt as marked. Outline quilt ¹/₄" from seam lines of the other patches. Bind to finish.

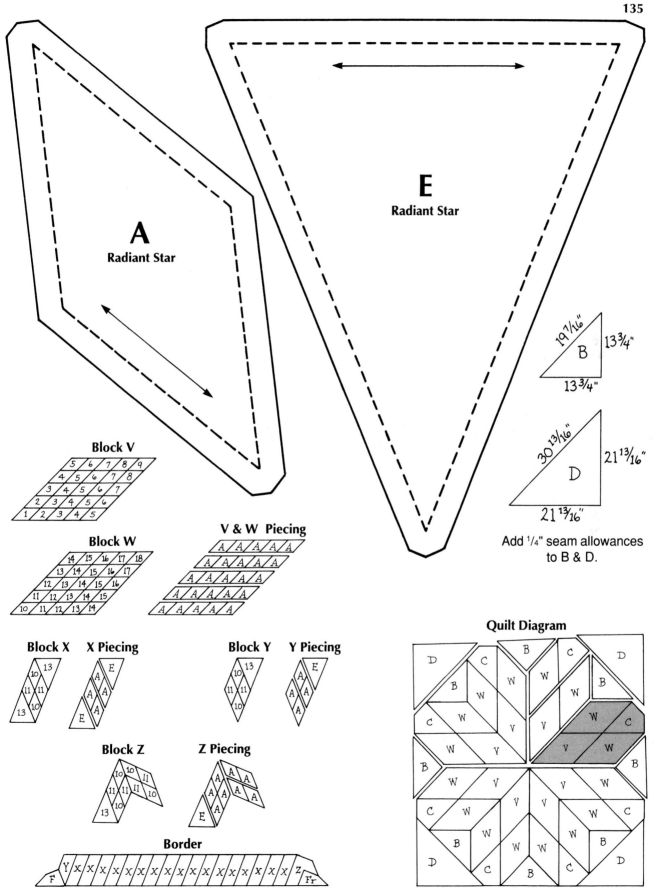

A
Radiant Star

E
Radiant Star

19⁷/₁₆" B 13³/₄"
13³/₄"

30¹³/₁₆" D 21¹³/₁₆"
21¹³/₁₆"

Add ¹/₄" seam allowances to B & D.

Block V

5	6	7	8	9
4	5	6	7	8
3	4	5	6	7
2	3	4	5	6
1	2	3	4	5

Block W

14	15	16	17	18
13	14	15	16	17
12	13	14	15	16
11	12	13	14	15
10	11	12	13	14

V & W Piecing

Block X **X Piecing**

Block Y **Y Piecing**

Block Z **Z Piecing**

Border

Quilt Diagram

Quilting for B

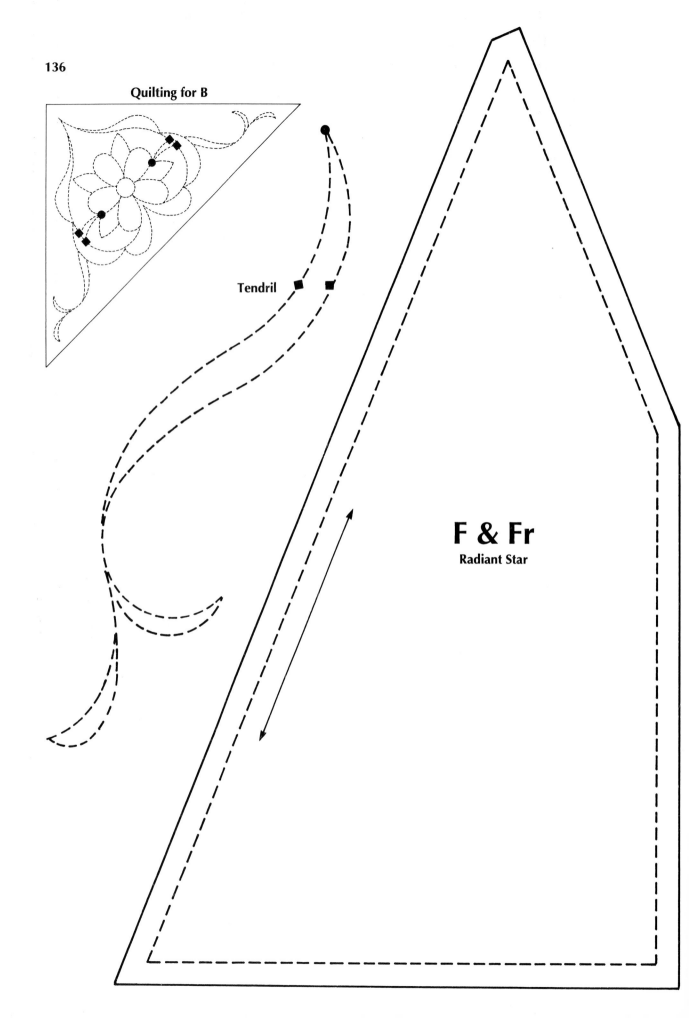

Tendril

F & Fr
Radiant Star

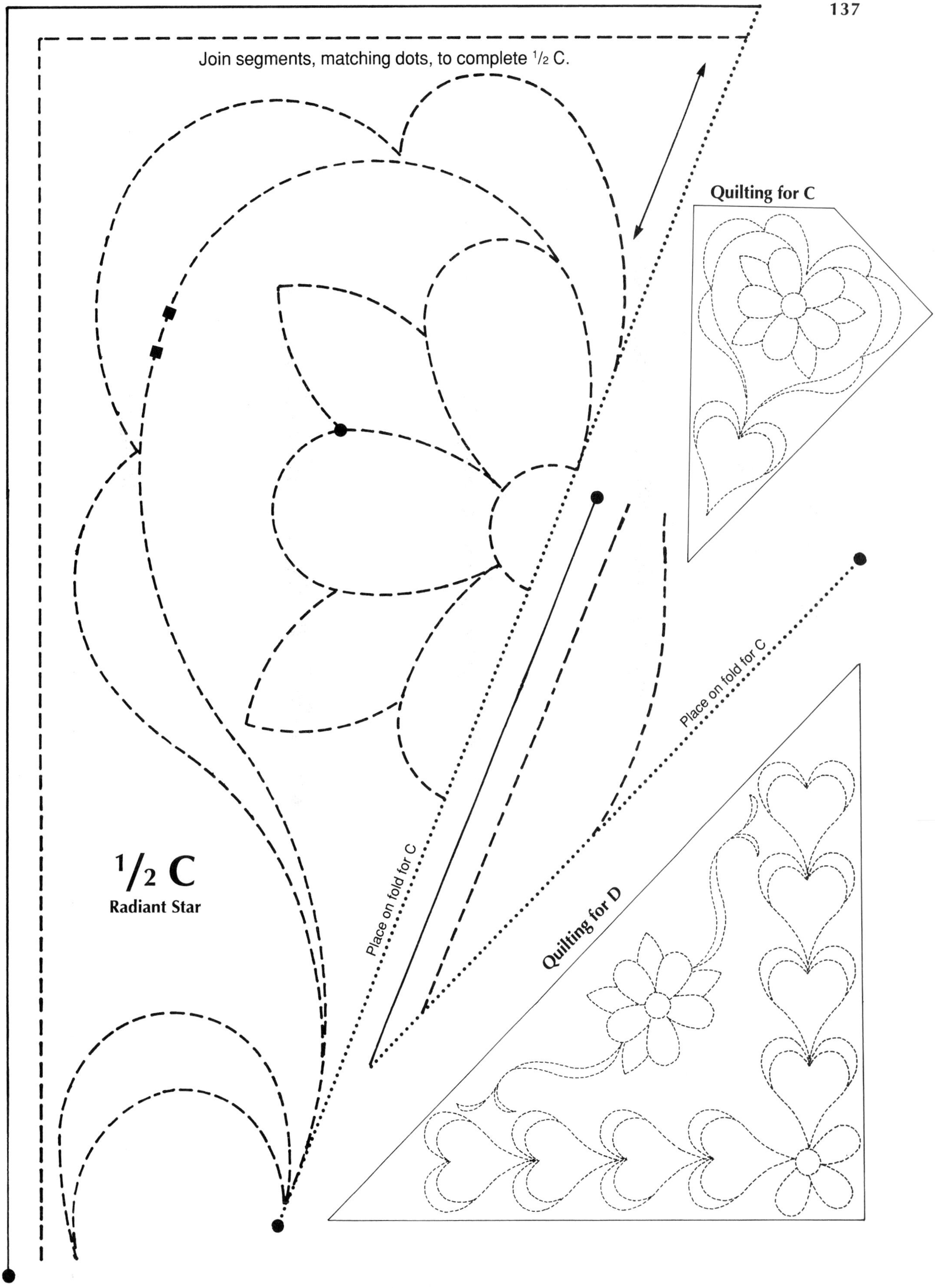

Join segments, matching dots, to complete ½ C.

Quilting for C

½ **C**
Radiant Star

Place on fold for C

Place on fold for C

Quilting for D

UNFOLDING STAR

Unfolding Star is arranged like a Stars and Cubes block. The star points are colored half light and half dark; the placement of lights and darks is meant to suggest folded star points highlighted by a light source. This quilt is shown in color on page 55.

HINT: To enhance the three-dimensional, "folded" effect that is just a subtle suggestion here, exaggerate the difference in shades between fabrics 2 and 3, 4 and 5, 6 and 7, and so forth.

Yardage (44" fabric) & Cutting Requirements

Diamond Size: $2^3/4$"
Quilt Size: $97^7/8$" x $97^7/8$"
$1^7/8$ yds. Fabric #1: binding
    $1^1/2$" x $11^1/2$ yds., 160 A
$1/4$ yd. Fabric #2: 16 A
$1/4$ yd. Fabric #3: 16A
$1/2$ yd. Fabric #4: 56 A
$1/2$ yd. Fabric #5: 56 A
$1/2$ yd. Fabric #6: 64 A
$1/2$ yd. Fabric #7: 64 A
$1/4$ yd. Fabric #8: 16 A
$1/2$ yd. Fabric #9: 64 A
$1/2$ yd. Fabric #10: 64 A
$1/2$ yd. Fabric #11: 64 A
$1/4$ yd. Fabric #12: 8 A
$1/4$ yd. Fabric #13: 8 A
$3/8$ yd. Fabric #14: 24 A
$3/8$ yd. Fabric #15: 24 A
$3/8$ yd. Fabric #16: 24 A
$3/8$ yd. Fabric #17: 24 A
$1/2$ yd. Fabric #18: 48 A
$1^5/8$ yds. Fabric #19: 8 B
$2^1/2$ yds. Fabric #20: 4 B, 8 C, 4 D
$2^7/8$ yds. Fabric #21:
    4 borders $2^1/2$" x $100^1/2$"
Batting: 102" x 102"
Lining: $8^3/4$ yds.

Referring to block coloring and piecing diagrams, make four W blocks, four X blocks, 12 Y blocks, and 12 Z blocks.

Join blocks, B's, C's, and D's as shown in the quilt diagram.

Referring to the figure on page 139, complete the quilting motif for the B square as follows: Trace the motif given on page 139 in each quarter of a $13^3/4$" square of paper. Leave off the curve labeled 1A in one quadrant and leave off 1B and 2 in the next quadrant. Add the flower and stem from page 140, matching dots and squares.

Referring to the figure on page 141, complete the quilting motif for D as follows: Trace the completed motif for B at one end of a $13^3/4$" x $27^1/2$" paper rectangle. Leave off the two end curls (#3 and #5). Turn the motif as shown and

repeat at the opposite end. Add the motif from page 141 at the center, aligning the center of the rectangle with the point where all of the curls meet. Also align the 4A curl from this motif with the 4A already drawn. Delete the 4B curl. To complete the motif for the C triangles, refer to the figure on page 141. Trace the 4A curl to complete the 4B curl.

Mark the completed motifs in B, C, and D patches. Quilt as marked and outline quilt the diamonds. Quilt the borders $1/4$" from long seam lines or quilt with a grid of squares or parallel lines as desired. Bind to finish.

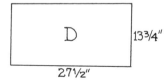

Add $1/4$" seam allowances to D.

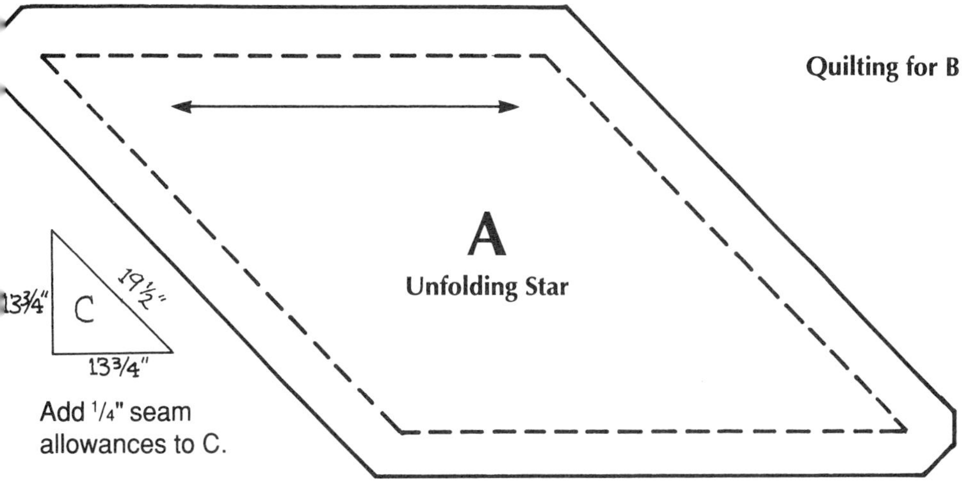

A

Unfolding Star

C

13¾"

19½"

13¾"

Add ¼" seam
allowances to C.

Quilting for B

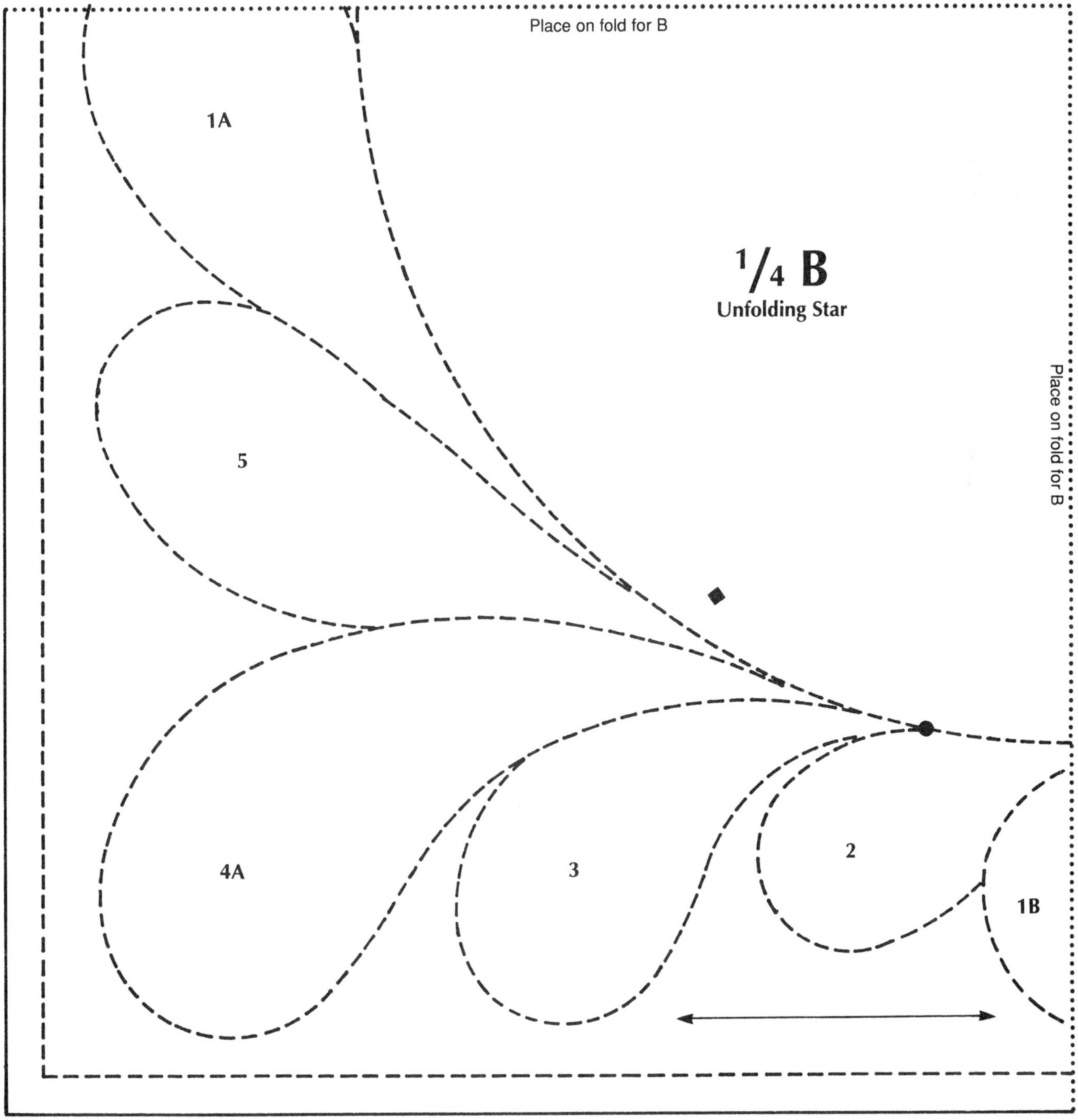

Place on fold for B

1A

¼ B

Unfolding Star

5

Place on fold for B

4A

3

2

1B

Quilt Diagram

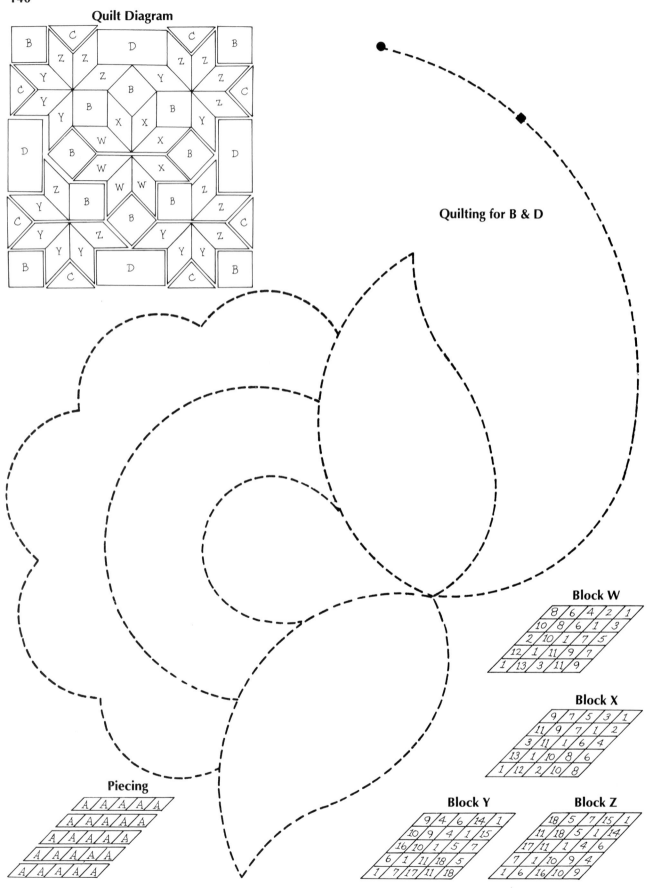

Quilting for B & D

Piecing

Block W

8	6	4	2	1
10	8	6	1	3
2	10	1	7	5
12	1	11	9	7
1	13	3	11	9

Block X

9	7	5	3	1
11	9	7	1	2
3	11	1	6	4
13	1	10	8	6
1	12	2	10	8

Block Y

9	4	6	14	1
10	9	4	1	15
16	10	1	5	7
6	1	11	18	5
1	7	17	11	18

Block Z

18	5	7	15	1
11	18	5	1	14
17	11	1	4	6
7	1	10	9	4
1	6	16	10	9

Quilting for C

Quilting for C & D

4B

141

Quilting for D

4A

BIBLIOGRAPHY

Albacete, M.J.; d'Atri, Sharon; and Reeves, Jane. *Ohio Quilts: A Living Tradition.* Canton, Ohio: The Canton Art Institute, 1981.

Andrews, Gail C., and McDonald, Janet Strain. *Alabama Quilts.* Birmingham: Birmingham Museum of Art, 1982.

Artistry in Quilts. Raleigh: North Carolina Museum of History, 1974.

Bacon, Lenice Ingram. *American Patchwork Quilts.* New York: William Morrow & Company, Inc., 1973.

Betterton, Shiela. *Quilts and Coverlets from the American Museum in Britain.* Bath: The American Museum in Britain, 1978.

Beyer, Jinny. *The Art and Technique of Creating Medallion Quilts.* McLean, Va.: EPM Publications, Inc., 1982.

Bishop, Robert. *New Discoveries in American Quilts.* New York: E.P. Dutton, Inc., 1975.

Bishop, Robert. *Quilts, Coverlets, Rugs, and Samplers.* New York: Alfred A. Knopf, 1982.

Bishop, Robert, and Safanda, Elizabeth. *A Gallery of Amish Quilts.* New York: E.P. Dutton, Inc., 1976.

Bordes, Marilynn Johnson. *12 Great Quilts from the American Wing.* New York: The Metropolitan Museum of Art, 1974.

Bullard, Lacy Folmar, and Shiell, Betty Jo. *Chintz Quilts: Unfading Glory.* Tallahassee: Serendipity Publishers, 1983.

Burnham, Dorothy K. *Pieced Quilts of Ontario.* Toronto: Royal Ontario Museum, 1975.

Carlisle, Lilian Baker. *Pieced Work and Applique Quilts at the Shelburne Museum.* Shelburne, Vt.: The Shelburne Museum, 1957.

A Century of Quilts from the Collections of the Oklahoma Historical Society. Oklahoma City: Oklahoma Historical Society, 1981.

Christopherson, Katy. *The Political and Campaign Quilt.* Frankfort: The Kentucky Heritage Quilt Society, 1984.

Clarke, Mary Washington. *Kentucky Quilts and Their Makers.* Lexington: The University Press of Kentucky, 1976.

Cooper, Patricia, and Buferd, Norma Bradley. *The Quilters, Women and Domestic Art.* Garden City, N.Y.: Doubleday and Co., Inc., 1977.

Curtis, Phillip H. "American Quilts in the Newark Museum Collection," *The Museum Series,* Vol. 25, Nos. 3 and 4, Summer/Fall, 1973. Newark: The Newark Museum Association, 1973.

Davison, Mildred. *American Quilts from The Art Institute of Chicago.* Chicago: The Art Institute of Chicago, 1966.

de Julio, Mary Antoine. *Quilts from Montgomery County, New York.* Fort Johnson, N.Y.: Montgomery County Historical Society, 1981.

Dubois, Jean. *A Galaxy of Stars: America's Favorite Quilts.* Fort Collins, Colo.: La Plata Press, 1976.

Finley, Ruth E. *Old Patchwork Quilts and the Women Who Made Them.* Philadelphia: J.P.Lippincott Company, 1929. Republished, Newton Centre, Mass.: Charles T. Branford Company, 1971.

Fox, Sandi. *Quilts in Utah, A Reflection of the Western Experience.* Salt Lake City: Salt Lake Art Center, 1981.

Fox, Sandi. *19th Century American Patchwork Quilt.* Tokyo: The Seibu Museum of Art, 1983.

LIST OF BOOKS AND CATALOGUES USED IN THE LONE STAR SURVEY

Gross, Joyce. *A Patch in Time.* Mill Valley, Calif.: The Mill Valley Quilt Authority, 1973.

Haders, Phyllis. *The Warner Collector's Guide to American Quilts.* New York: The Main Street Press, 1981.

Holstein, Jonathan. *American Pieced Quilts.* New York: The Viking Press, 1972.

Holstein, Jonathan, and Finley, John. *Kentucky Quilts 1800-1900.* Louisville: The Kentucky Quilt Project, 1982.

Horton, Laurel, and Myers, Lynn Robertson. *Social Fabric, South Carolina's Traditional Quilts.* Columbia: McKissick Museum, The University of South Carolina, 1985.

Houck, Carter, and Miller, Myron. *American Quilts and How To Make Them.* New York: Charles Scribner's Sons, 1975.

Irwin, John Rice. *A People and Their Quilts.* Exton, Pa.: Schiffer Publishing Ltd., 1983.

Johnson, Bruce. *A Child's Comfort, Baby and Doll Quilts in American Folk Art.* New York: Harcourt Brace Jovanovich, 1977.

Kiracofe, Roderick, and Kile, Michael. *The Quilt Digest.* San Francisco: Quilt Digest Press, 1983.

Kiracofe, Roderick, and Kile, Michael. *The Quilt Digest 2.* San Francisco: Quilt Digest Press, 1984.

Lasansky, Jeannette. *In the Heart of Pennsylvania, 19th and 20th Century Quiltmaking Traditions.* Lewisburg, Pa.: Oral Traditions Project, 1985.

Lasansky, Jeannette. *In the Heart of Pennsylvania, Symposium Papers.* Lewisburg, Pa.: Oral Traditions Project, 1986.

McKendry, Ruth. *Traditional Quilts and Bed Coverings.* New York: Van Nostrand Reinhold Company, 1979.

Merriam, Mary, and Flynt, Suzanne L. *Quilts.* Deerfield, Mass.: Pocumtock Valley Memorial Association, 1985.

Nelson, Cyril I., and Houck, Carter. *The Quilt Engagement Calendar Treasury.* New York: E. P. Dutton, Inc., 1982.

North Carolina Country Quilts: Regional Variations. Chapel Hill: The Ackland Art Museum, University of North Carolina at Chapel Hill, 1978.

Old Line Traditions, Maryland Women and Their Quilts. Washington, D.C.: DAR Museum, 1985.

Orlofsky, Patsy and Myron. *Quilts in America.* New York: McGraw-Hill Book Company, 1974.

Pottinger, David. *Quilts from the Indiana Amish, A Regional Collection.* New York: E.P. Dutton, Inc.,1983.

Quilt Close-Up: Five Southern Views. Chattanooga, Tenn.: The Hunter Museum of Art, 1983.

Quilters' Choice, Quilts from the Museum Collection. Lawrence: Helen Foresman Spencer Museum of Art, The University of Kansas, Lawrence, 1978.

Quilts from Nebraska Collections. Lincoln: Sheldon Memorial Art Gallery, University of Nebraska-Lincoln, 1974.

Ramsey, Bets, and Waldvogel, Merikay. *The Quilts of Tennessee, Images of Domestic Life Prior to 1930.* Nashville: Rutledge Hill Press, 1986.

Safford, Carleton L., and Bishop, Robert. *America's Quilts and Coverlets.* New York: Weathervane Books, 1974.

Shine, Carolyn R. *Quilts from Cincinnati Collections.* Cincinnati: Cincinnati

Art Museum, 1985.

200 Years of American Quilts in Illinois Private Collections. Normal: Center for the Visual Arts Gallery, Illinois State University, Normal, 1976.

Webster, Marie D. *Quilts, Their Story and How to Make Them.* New York: Doubleday, Page, and Company, 1915.

Woodard, Thos. K., and Greenstein, Blanche. *Crib Quilts and Other Small Wonders.* New York: E. P. Dutton, Inc., 1981.

World of Quilts at Meadow Brook Hall. Rochester, Mich.: privately published, 1983.

Yabsley, Suzanne. *Texas Quilts, Texas Women.* College Station: Texas A & M University Press, 1984.

OTHER BOOKS OF INTEREST FROM MOON OVER THE MOUNTAIN PUBLISHING COMPANY

Keeping It All Together, The Not-Just-For-Quiltmakers Coping Book by Jean Ray Laury

Log Cabin Quilts by Bonnie Leman and Judy Martin

Taking the Math Out of Making Patchwork Quilts by Bonnie Leman and Judy Martin

How To Make a Quilt, 25 Easy Lessons for Beginners by Bonnie Leman and Louise O. Townsend

Patchwork Sampler Legacy Quilt, Intermediate and Advanced Lessons in Patchwork by Bonnie Leman and the Staff of *Quilter's Newsletter Magazine*

The Rainbow Collection, Quilt Patterns for Rainbow Colors by Judy Martin

Scrap Quilts by Judy Martin

First Aid For Family Quilts by Nancy O'Bryant Puentes

RESOURCES

The QuickStar tool, Rainbow Collection fabrics, and other supplies mentioned in this book are available at quilt shops throughout the United States and other countries. They can also be ordered directly from Quilts & Other Comforts, 6700-A West 44th Avenue, Wheatridge, Colorado 80034-0394. Send $2.50 for fabric swatches and 32-page catalog.